Ancient Greece

Peter Ackroyd

LONDON, NEW YORK, MUNICH,
MELBOURNE, and DELHI

Project editor Hazel Beynon
Editor Susan Kennedy
Designers Kavita Dutta, Arunesh Talapatra
Managing art editor Diane Thistlethwaite
Senior editor David John
Managing editor Linda Esposito
Publishing managers Caroline Buckingham, Andrew Macintyre
Art director Simon Webb
Publishing director Jonathan Metcalf
Production controller Luca Bazzoli
DTP designer Siu Yin Ho
DK Cartography Paul Eames
Picture researcher Sarah Pownall
Picture librarians Rose Horridge, Kate Ledwith, Sarah Mills
Jacket designer Neal Cobourne

Consultant
Dr Hugh Bowden

First published in Great Britain in 2005 by
Dorling Kindersley Limited
80 Strand, London WC2R 0RL

A Penguin Company

2 4 6 8 10 9 7 5 3 1

A CIP catalogue record for this book is available from the British Library.

ISBN 1 4053 0733 1

Reproduced by Colourscan
Printed and bound in China by Hung Hing

See our complete catalogue at
www.dk.com

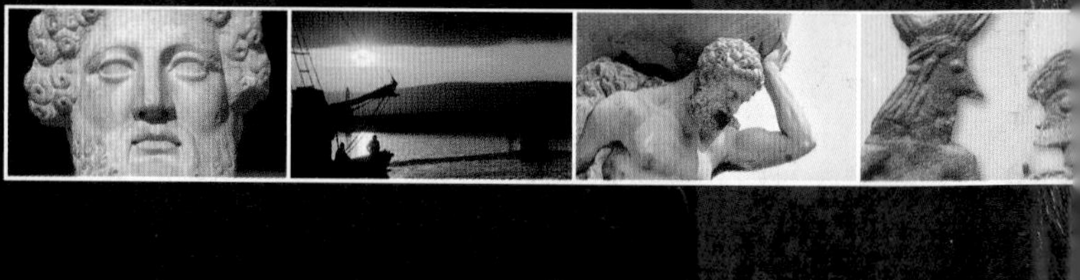

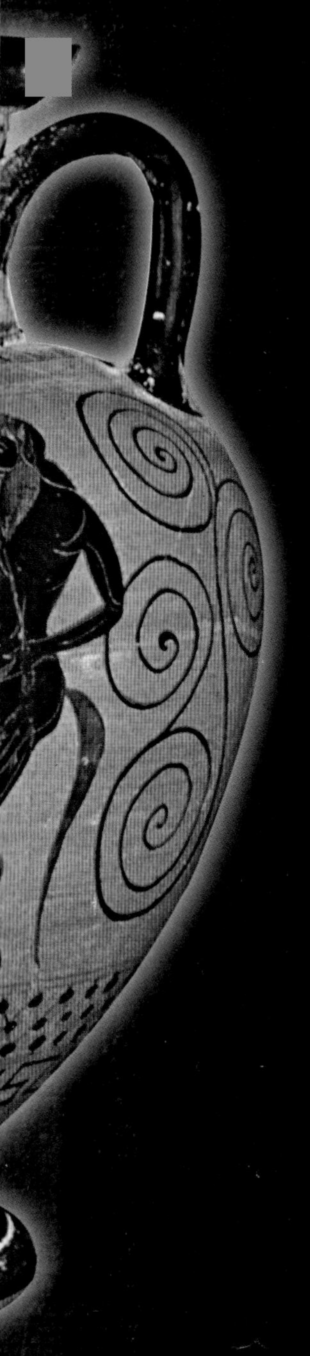

Contents

From ancient Greece came **ideas and beliefs** that still influence how we think and behave.

More than two thousand years ago, the people of Greece developed one of the most advanced civilizations of the ancient world. The ancient Greeks invented democracy. They discovered physics and geography. They were the first people to write history, comedy and tragedy and to ask questions about the world. How does the universe work? How should children be educated? Can war be justified? They called this philosophy, which simply means the love of wisdom.

One great legacy of the ancient Greeks is athletics – the Olympic Games were first held in Greece almost 3,000 years ago. And, in architecture and in art, the Greeks created the "classical" style. Their marble columns and lifelike carved statues are still seen today in the public buildings of every capital city of the world. We take these things for granted – they are a part of our lives – but they were the achievements and inventions of the Greeks.

If you look at some of the English words that have come to us from Greek, you can begin to understand the importance of this ancient civilization. Scholars estimate that a third of modern English words come from Greek originals, an astonishing number for a language first spoken thousands of years ago. The Greeks have given us such words as politician and actor, architect and acrobat, hero and heretic, museum and atom, physics and economics. The list reaches into almost every aspect of our daily lives.

So how did this great civilization develop in the southeastern corner of Europe many centuries ago? The landscape must have played some part. The Greek mainland is very mountainous, with many small valleys closed off from one another by rocky terrain. That may help to account for the independence of the Greek spirit. The world of the Greeks also consisted of jagged coastline and extended across the numerous islands of the Aegean Sea to the west coast of Turkey, known in ancient times as Asia Minor. One famous philosopher, whose name was Plato, said that all the Greeks around the coasts and on the islands were like "frogs around a pond".

Although the Greek cities were separated from each other by mountain ranges and by the sea, the Greeks had a common language, although they spoke different dialects. They also shared many gods and goddesses and the same myths and legends. They thought that the best kind of life was to be found in the city, and that war was a necessary and inevitable part of life.

Living by the sea made the Greeks travel and explore. It gave them curiosity. Since the sea was by far the best means of travelling, the Greeks made many journeys to the south and to the east, where they encountered much older civilizations than their own. They went on to found cities around the shores of the Mediterranean and the Black Sea, where the the Greek way of life flourished. The influence of Greek culture spread throughout the ancient world, and it still influences how we think and behave today.

CHAPTER ONE

The age of the kings

The origins of the Greek people lie far back in the period of time known as prehistory. The first Greeks were Stone-Age people who did not settle, but wandered from place to place hunting wild animals and gathering wild plants.

THESE EARLY HUMANS USED tools made of bone and stone and lived in caves or in shelters made from the branches of trees. Between 8,000 and 7,000 years ago, people living in the fertile areas of Greece gradually gave up the life of wandering and hunting. They settled down and started to grow crops of wheat and barley. They tended sheep and goats, and they built houses of mud bricks with thatched roofs. Their small settlements and farms gradually developed into villages. But the most important change occurred in about 3000 BCE, when the early Greeks learned how to make bronze by melting copper and mixing it with another metal, usually tin. Over time, tools and weapons of stone were replaced by stronger ones of bronze and copper. Bronze was also used to make valuable household articles, such as jewellery, cups and bowls.

◄ Temple of Poseidon at Sounion, Greece

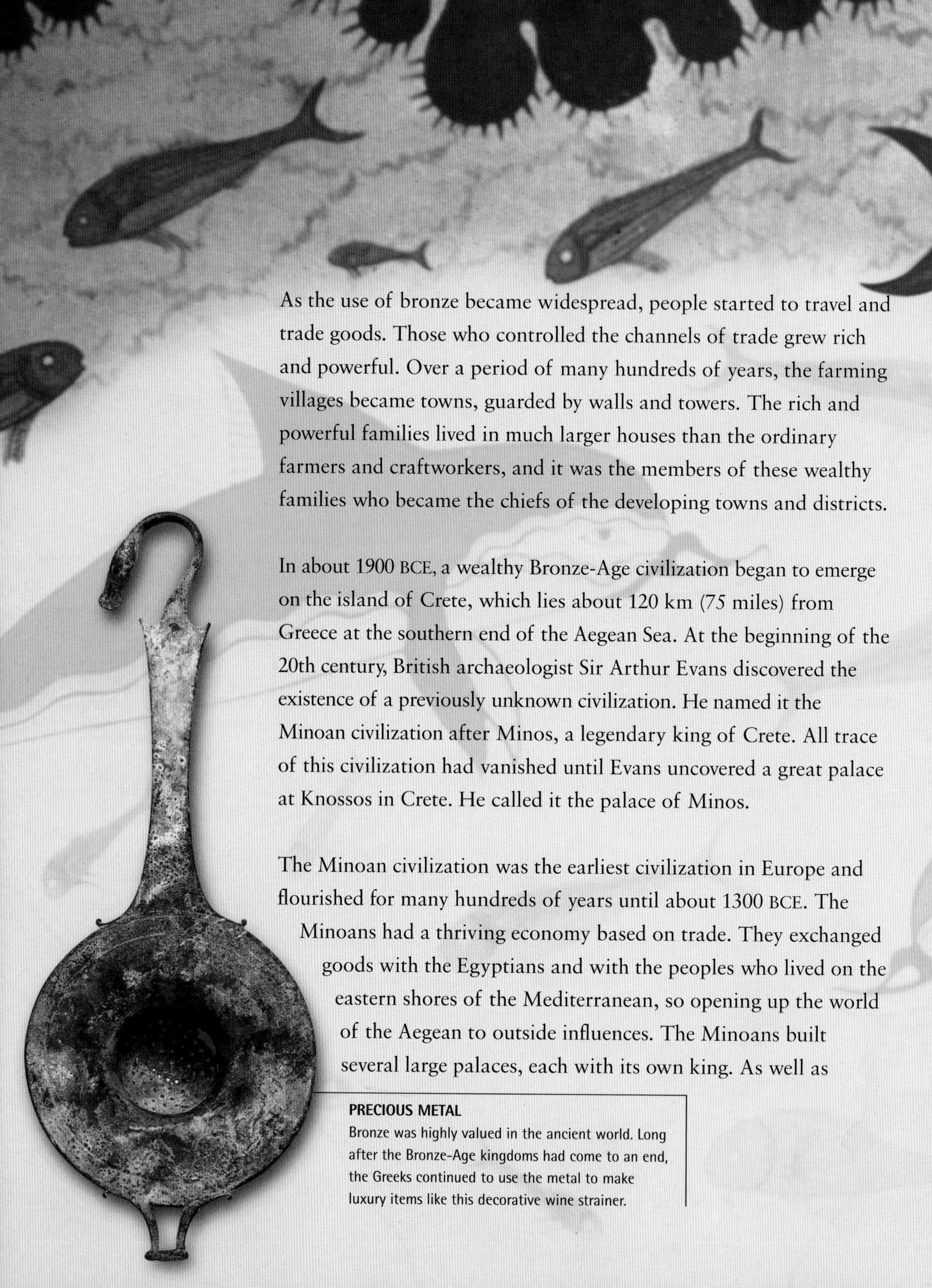

As the use of bronze became widespread, people started to travel and trade goods. Those who controlled the channels of trade grew rich and powerful. Over a period of many hundreds of years, the farming villages became towns, guarded by walls and towers. The rich and powerful families lived in much larger houses than the ordinary farmers and craftworkers, and it was the members of these wealthy families who became the chiefs of the developing towns and districts.

In about 1900 BCE, a wealthy Bronze-Age civilization began to emerge on the island of Crete, which lies about 120 km (75 miles) from Greece at the southern end of the Aegean Sea. At the beginning of the 20th century, British archaeologist Sir Arthur Evans discovered the existence of a previously unknown civilization. He named it the Minoan civilization after Minos, a legendary king of Crete. All trace of this civilization had vanished until Evans uncovered a great palace at Knossos in Crete. He called it the palace of Minos.

The Minoan civilization was the earliest civilization in Europe and flourished for many hundreds of years until about 1300 BCE. The Minoans had a thriving economy based on trade. They exchanged goods with the Egyptians and with the peoples who lived on the eastern shores of the Mediterranean, so opening up the world of the Aegean to outside influences. The Minoans built several large palaces, each with its own king. As well as

PRECIOUS METAL
Bronze was highly valued in the ancient world. Long after the Bronze-Age kingdoms had come to an end, the Greeks continued to use the metal to make luxury items like this decorative wine strainer.

Knossos, archaeologists have excavated three other large palaces and several smaller ones on Crete. It appears that the ruling elite lived in the palaces, while the rest of the population lived in the towns that clustered around them.

The royal palaces were very luxurious with colourful balconies and verandas. The Minoans had baths and flushing toilets, and the water for washing and drinking was fed through an elaborate system of pipes. Many rooms in the palace at Knossos were decorated with lavish wall paintings known as frescoes, which give us a fascinating insight into Minoan life and religious worship.

LEAPING DOLPHINS
The Minoans took great delight in the natural world around them. These lively dolphins are from a fresco in the queen's apartment at Knossos.

The palace at Knossos

The vast palace at Knossos was like a busy beehive, humming with activity. Towering stone buildings, sometimes six storeys high, stood around a large central courtyard. These buildings contained hundreds of rooms. Grain and olive oil, products of the rich Cretan soil, were kept in huge pottery jars in large storage rooms on the ground floor. Other rooms were used as workshops or religious shrines. Many rooms housed the scribes who were responsible for overseeing the business of the palace. Finally, there were the grand public areas and decorated apartments for the ruling elite.

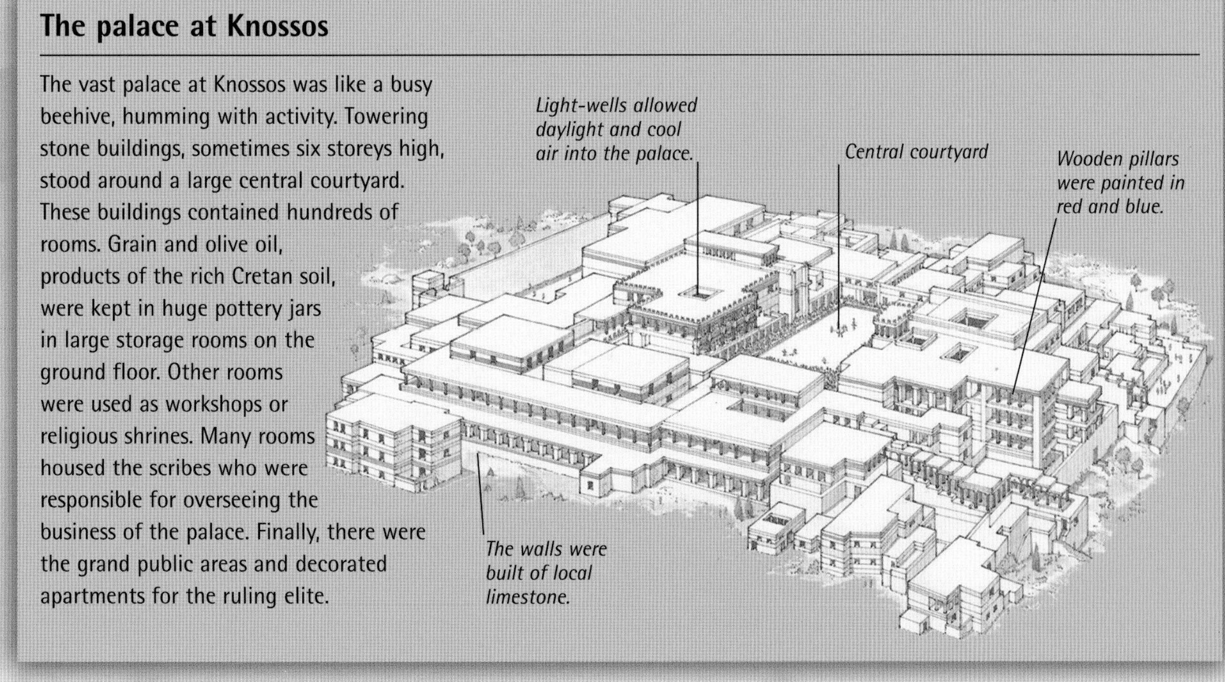

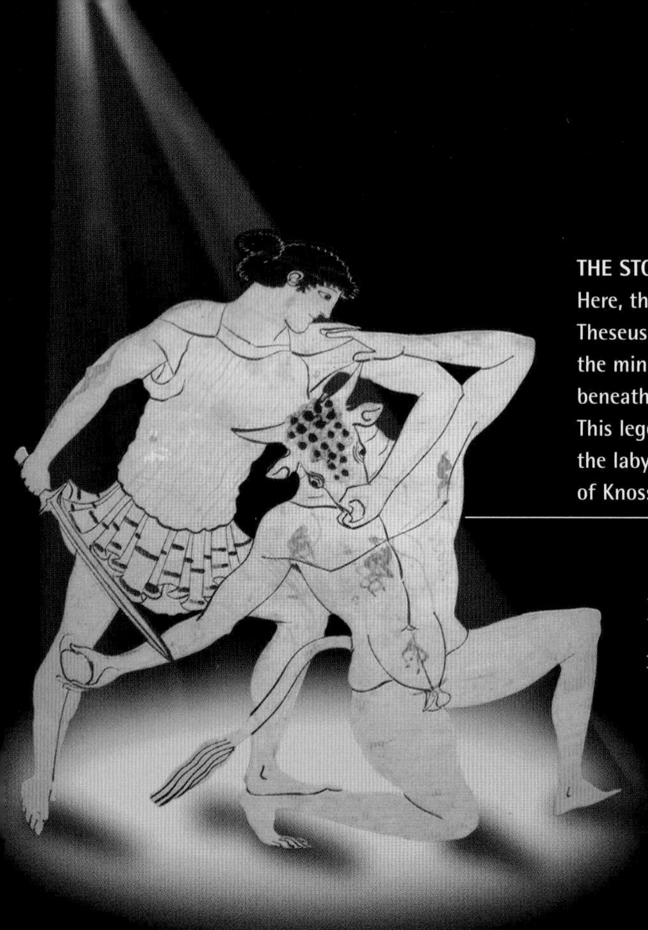

THE STORY OF THESEUS
Here, the Greek hero Theseus is shown killing the minotaur in the maze beneath Minos's palace. This legend may refer to the labyrinth-like layout of Knossos itself.

But there were darker aspects to Minoan life. According to Greek myth, the palace of King Minos contained a great maze, or labyrinth, of stone passages, through which it was impossible to find one's way. In this labyrinth lived the minotaur, a terrible man-eating monster with a man's body and a bull's head.

Legend says that King Minos captured young men and women and walled them up inside the labyrinth to wander through the corridors of stone, completely lost and bewildered, until the minotaur found and devoured them.

SNAKE GODDESS
This figurine of painted ivory is often called the Snake Goddess, although she may be a priestess. She is holding a snake in each hand and has a bird on her head.

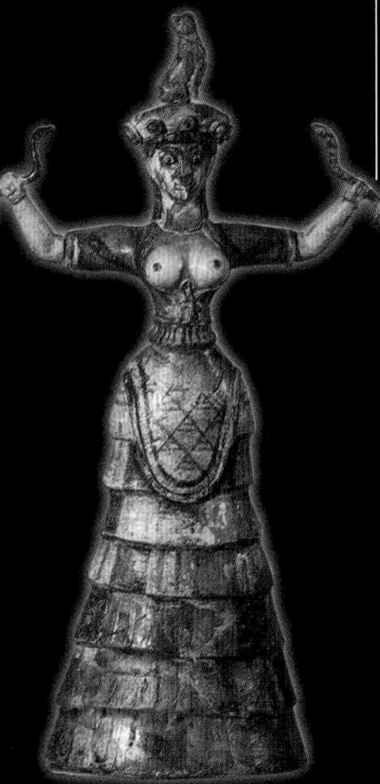

We know little about the religion of the Minoans, but there is some evidence to suggest that they practised human sacrifice. Many Minoan paintings show images of bulls and of athletes taking part in the dangerous sport of bull-leaping (jumping over bulls' backs). It is likely that the Minoans regarded bulls as sacred, and bull-leaping may have been part of a religious ritual. We know from paintings and statues that the Minoans regarded caves and mountain tops as sacred places. We also know that they worshipped a number of goddesses, one of whom is known as the Mistress of the Animals, another as the Snake Goddess.

One of the most notable achievements of the Minoan people was the development of at least two systems of writing. At first, they used a form of hieroglyphs (picture writing). Later, in about 2000 BCE, they developed a script known as Linear A, which was made up of signs and pictures. To this day, no one has been able to decipher these scripts. The writing was scratched onto clay tablets, which archaeologists believe were a way of recording details of the food and other goods stored in the palace warehouses. There would have been palace officials and scribes to keep the records and accounts up to date.

The world of the Minoans was highly organized. It appears that the palaces were not fortified, so the early Minoans probably lived in a peaceful society, with no obvious threat of war. The decline of the Minoan civilization may have started with a series of earthquakes or volcanic eruptions. By about 1450 BCE, the Minoan culture had collapsed, and the palaces had been destroyed by fire. It seems that the island was invaded and conquered by people from the Greek mainland. These invaders were known as the Mycenaeans.

The Mycenaeans had settled on mainland Greece in about 2000 BCE. They were named after a famous fortress-palace at a place called Mycenae. The Mycenaeans lived in small independent kingdoms, each based round a separate city. Mycenae was thought to have been the richest and most powerful of these kingdoms.

MYSTERIOUS DISC
This baked clay disc from southern Crete is stamped with a unique form of writing that may represent a third Minoan script.

ALL AT SEA
This fresco from a Minoan settlement on the Aegean island of Thera shows ships leaving the harbour, watched by crowds of people on the shore.

ANCIENT WEAPON
Once the property of a Mycenaean warrior, this bronze dagger is about 3,600 years old. The blade is decorated with an intricate design in silver.

FACE OF A KING
Several of the Mycenaean kings were buried with gold funeral masks placed over their faces. This mask was once mistakenly thought to have been the death mask of King Agamemnon.

The earliest evidence we have of the Mycenaean civilization is from the royal tombs at Mycenae, which were discovered in the 19th century. There, archaeologists found great stone-lined grave pits (known as shaft-graves) dating from about 1650 BCE. The Mycenaeans believed in life after death and buried their dead with jewels, weapons and other artefacts for the next life. Later, in about 1500 BCE, members of the royal family were buried in graves known as beehive tombs, which were underground dome-shaped stone chambers, reached by a tunnel.

The Mycenaean royal families lived in palaces, built around a large central room known as a *megaron*, in which there was a central hearth and a throne. The king was called the *wanax*, and he ruled a society of priests, warriors, craftworkers and slaves. The Mycenaean culture was one of fighting, raiding and hunting – the palace walls were painted with scenes of battles and boar-hunts, lions and spearmen. Soldiers wore complete body armour of bronze, together with shields of leather and boar-tusk helmets. Some of their warriors fought in two-wheeled chariots pulled by two horses.

After the conquest of Crete, the Mycenaeans became active traders throughout the eastern Mediterranean. They had outposts in Crete and on the islands of the Aegean Sea. They traded across the sea as far as Egypt, and there is evidence of Mycenaean pottery and other goods at sites in the Middle East. But their heartland was in central and southern Greece, and as the Mycenaean kings became wealthier through trade, their palaces became larger and more strongly fortified. The walls were built of great stone blocks, so huge that the later Greeks believed that only giants could have lifted them.

LION GATE
This fortress-palace, or citadel, of Mycenae was surrounded by a wall built of massive stone blocks. Two stone lions, headless now, stood guard above the great gateway.

These buildings became known as Cyclopean, named after Cyclops, the legendary one-eyed giant.

The Mycenaeans adapted the writing systems of the Minoans and devised their own script known as Linear B. Clay tablets written in Linear B were found at Knossos on Crete and at many sites in Greece and the Aegean. For centuries, no one could read the script, and the language of the Mycenaeans remained a mystery. Then, in 1952, a young Englishman named Michael Ventris managed to decipher the signs. Much to the astonishment of scholars, he showed that Linear B represented an early form of Greek. So the language of the Mycenaeans was the ancestor of classical Greek and has descended in a long line to the language spoken in Greece today. The tablets contained mostly lists made by chariot-makers, carpenters, goldsmiths and weavers, recording details of exports such as furniture and cloth.

VASE OF TENTACLES
The Mycenaeans traded all over the eastern Mediterranean. This vase, decorated with an octopus, comes from a settlement in Rhodes. The swirling pattern of the tentacles is typical of Mycenaean art.

The impression of Mycenaean wealth is borne out by many archaeological finds from the palaces, including chairs and footstools, mirrors and musical instruments, stone lamps and ivory figures, and large amounts of pottery. There is also, of course, much bronze, the great and indispensable

EARLY GODS
The Mycenaeans already worshipped some of the gods of the later Greeks, such as Poseidon, the god of the sea, and Zeus, the sky-god (shown below).

metal of the Mycenaean kings. The tablets also tell us of the gods worshipped by the Mycenaeans. Religion was a central part of Greek life, even in early times.

But the Mycenaean civilization itself did not last. From the 13th century BCE, trade decreased, and the rich and powerful centres of Mycenaean Greece entered a period of decline, if not outright destruction. Some historians believe that Greece was disrupted by a great natural disaster, such as an earthquake or a catastrophic crop failure. Others have speculated that the Mycenaean civilization was destroyed from within, and that the kingdoms fought against each other with such ferocity that they destroyed each other. We will probably never know the truth.

Archaeologists have discovered that many cities and towns in the eastern Mediterranean were destroyed at this time, and that the empire of the Hittites, in present-day Turkey, also ended suddenly. There were upheavals in Mesopotamia, and we know that, during this period, mysterious invaders called the Sea Peoples fought great battles against the Egyptians. It seems possible that the destruction of the Mycenaean civilization was connected in some way with the events of these troubled times.

And so the Mycenaean kings were destroyed without leaving a trace in any recorded history. They may have remained as distant legends and figures of myth in ancient Greek poetry, which looked back to a vanished age of heroes. The legends of

EARLY GREEK WRITING
The scratched marks on this clay tablet are the Linear B script of the Mycenaeans, now known to be an early form of Greek writing.

DESPERATE TIMES
Raids by the Sea Peoples, seen here on an Egyptian carving, were part of a wave of violence in the Near East. The Sea Peoples launched two attacks on the Egyptians but were beaten off both times.

Heracles, or of Jason and the Argonauts, for example, may have a grain of historical fact behind them. We do not need to believe in all the details of their fabulous adventures, but the poems and songs that record their deeds may contain traces of real events and wars that happened centuries ago.

The most famous legend of all concerned an ancient war between the Greeks and a city called Troy on the coast of Asia Minor. Legend tells that a prince of Troy kidnapped a beautiful Greek queen named Helen. In revenge, the Greeks, led by King Agamemnon, decided to sail to Troy and besiege the city. For ten years, the Greeks fought against the Trojans, led by King Priam and his son, Hector. Finally, the Greek hero Odysseus devised a plan in which he concealed some of the Greek warriors in a wooden horse. It was a clever trick. The Trojans thought the horse was a peace offering from the surrendering army and dragged it inside their city. Then, the Greek soldiers leapt out of the horse, killed the guards and threw open the city gates to let in the Greek army. Soon, the great city was in flames, and the ten-year war was over.

LABOURS OF HERACLES
Heracles was made to perform 12 impossible tasks, including killing a flock of birds that fed on human flesh.

HELEN AND MENELAUS
This carving shows Helen of Troy with her husband Menelaus, king of Sparta. Helen is often described as "the face that launched a thousand ships" on account of her beauty.

These stories were not written down until the 8th century BCE. However, in the 19th century, a German adventurer named Heinrich Schliemann fell in love with Greek poetry, and especially with the story of the Trojan War. He trusted the words of the poets who had written of Agamemnon and of Priam, king of Troy. He dreamed of finding the vanished city of Troy and began digging at a site in Turkey. There he found evidence of a Bronze-Age city, which he believed was the one destroyed by the Greeks. He excavated several sites in Greece, including Mycenae. And there, by an extraordinary piece of luck, he found

TROJAN HORSE
Most historians doubt whether there was a real Trojan war, but the story of the wooden horse still fascinates us today.

some shaft-graves containing treasures and weapons.

Schliemann made many mistakes – for example, there is no evidence to link the story of Agamemnon to Mycenae. But, before his discoveries, this distant period of Greek history was known to no one. Thanks to Heinrich Schliemann and the archaeologists who followed him, we now have a fascinating insight into the lost world of the Mycenaeans.

TROJAN TREASURE
Heinrich Schliemann found many pieces of superb jewellery while excavating the site at Troy. He claimed that this beautiful earring, made of silver and gold, had once graced the ear of Helen of Troy.

After the destruction of the Mycenaean civilization in about 1200 BCE, Greece entered a period known as the Dark Age. During this time, the Greeks lost the art of writing. No new palaces were built, trade decreased and many traditional skills died out.

THERE WAS A MASSIVE FALL in population, perhaps by as much as 60 to 90 per cent in some regions. This population loss is far larger than that during the Black Death, the plague that killed a third of the population of Europe in the 14th century CE. It was probably caused by famine or warfare, but as no written records survive from this period, we do not really know why it happened. Of course, no "Dark Age" is dark to the people who live in it. People still had to grow wheat and barley, look after their sheep and cattle, build houses and make tools. But the Dark Age appears to have been a time of shrunken horizons, when people lived in small self-enclosed communities with little interest in the outside world. This period in Greek history lasted for about 300 years, but it would be absurd to think of 300 years as wholly wasted or without interest.

◀ A Greek ship moors in a harbour in the Aegean Sea at sunset

BURNT OFFERING
This vase painting shows a sacrifice to the goddess Athena, who is standing by the altar. A girl presents ears of wheat, while three young men lead an ox to be killed and burned at the altar.

People continued to speak Greek, the language spoken by the Mycenaeans, and they still worshipped some of the same gods. Religion was central to the lives of these early Greeks. They believed that the gods and goddesses played an active role in their lives and that it was important to win their support. To please the gods, the Greeks carried out various rites and ceremonies. They honoured the gods who dwelled above the earth with open-air sacrifices. The fat and bones of slaughtered sheep or oxen were burned on an altar so that the rising smoke could carry the offering up through the air. The rest of the meat was cooked and eaten by the human worshippers. The Greeks also worshipped the mysterious gods of the Underworld, who lived beneath the earth. They honoured these gods by pouring wine and animal blood onto the ground. Certain places in the landscape, such as clefts in the rock, were thought to be entrances to the Underworld, where it was possible for humans to communicate with these dark gods, and with the dead.

The Dark Age witnessed one change that was of immense importance – the replacement of bronze by iron. The invention of iron-working was one of the great advances in world technology, equivalent to the invention of the wheel or the advent of human flight. It involved a complicated process of cooling and reheating the metal before cooling it again. The skill was not discovered in Greece, but arrived from further east some time after 1000 BCE. But the practice of iron-making spread quickly through Greece, and tools and weapons made of iron began to be widely used.

BLACKSMITH AT WORK
The blacksmith put the crushed ore – pieces of rock containing iron – inside a furnace. He used bellows to fan the burning charcoal until the temperature was high enough to melt the metal, which formed a soft lump. Here, the smith is removing the lump of iron from the furnace with a pair of tongs, ready for the anvil.

One intriguing glimpse of life in the Dark Age emerged on the island of Euboea (now Evia), off the coast of eastern Greece. Here, archaeologists discovered the remains of a strange building. It was built in the 10th century BCE, in the middle of the Dark Age, and it bears no relationship to earlier Mycenaean buildings. It is in the shape of a large rectangle, 45 m (147 ft) long and 10 m (32 ft) wide. Inside, archaeologists found a tomb with two different compartments – in one of them were the remains of a man and woman, and in the other were the skeletons of four horses. It may have been a tomb for an important couple, perhaps the leaders of the local community, but their identity and the actual purpose of the large building remain a mystery. However, succeeding generations chose to bury their dead around the mound that covered the

MAKING A SWORD
As the blacksmith hammered the hot iron on his anvil, it became thinner and harder. He plunged the iron into cold water, reheated it in his fire, and hammered it again, repeating each step until he had a strong, sharp blade.

PERFUME FROM CORINTH
This pot once held perfume and was made in Corinth, a town that became famous for its novelty perfume pots. This pot would have had a wax stopper to prevent the perfume from evaporating.

place where the building had stood. Some of the goods placed in these graves came from overseas, which suggests that the people of this area were trading with merchants from the east. So it seems that Greece may not have been entirely isolated through its Dark Age. As early as 1000 BCE, Greek settlements began to appear on the islands of the Aegean Sea and on the coast of Asia Minor (now Turkey). The Greeks knew this region as Ionia and, in later times, it became one of the most advanced and interesting areas of Greece.

By the 9th century BCE, there were signs that Greece was recovering. Trade grew with other parts of the Mediterranean world, and Greek towns and cities came into increasing contact with one another. It was around this time that the first Greek temples were built. These were not the gleaming stone temples of later periods, but small buildings with mud-brick walls and thatched roofs. In the centre, was a hearth or altar for sacrifices.

GEOMETRIC DESIGNS
Between the 10th and 8th centuries BCE, new forms of pottery started to appear. It was fashionable to decorate Greek pots with geometric designs of stripes, zigzags and triangles.

MYTHOLOGICAL BEAST
This terracotta statuette of a centaur – a beast with the front half of a man and the back half of a horse – was found in the cemetery of Lefkandi on the island of Euboea.

NEW SETTLEMENTS
Greeks leaving the mainland were driven by poverty, war, famine and overcrowding. This stretch of Ionian coastline (now part of Turkey) looks much the same as it did when the Greeks first settled here.

In this period, it seems likely that all the villages or towns within a particular territory were ruled by a council of local chieftains, possibly led by a single man. Each town had its own assembly made up of the men in the community. There was probably also a system of justice for settling disputes, in which the local chiefs would play a large part. As conditions continued to improve in the 8th century BCE, the population of Greece started to rise. Agricultural land had to be used more intensively in order to feed the growing population, and landowners played an increasingly important role in society. Over time, the power of individual leaders gave way to the power of the aristocracy – the group of people made up of rich and powerful landowners and the military elite.

With increased wealth, cities began to grow. The aristocrats were responsible for making and maintaining the laws, for preserving the rituals and festivals of the religious year, and for filling the most important political offices in the city and its surrounding territory. Beneath them were the farmers and the craftworkers.

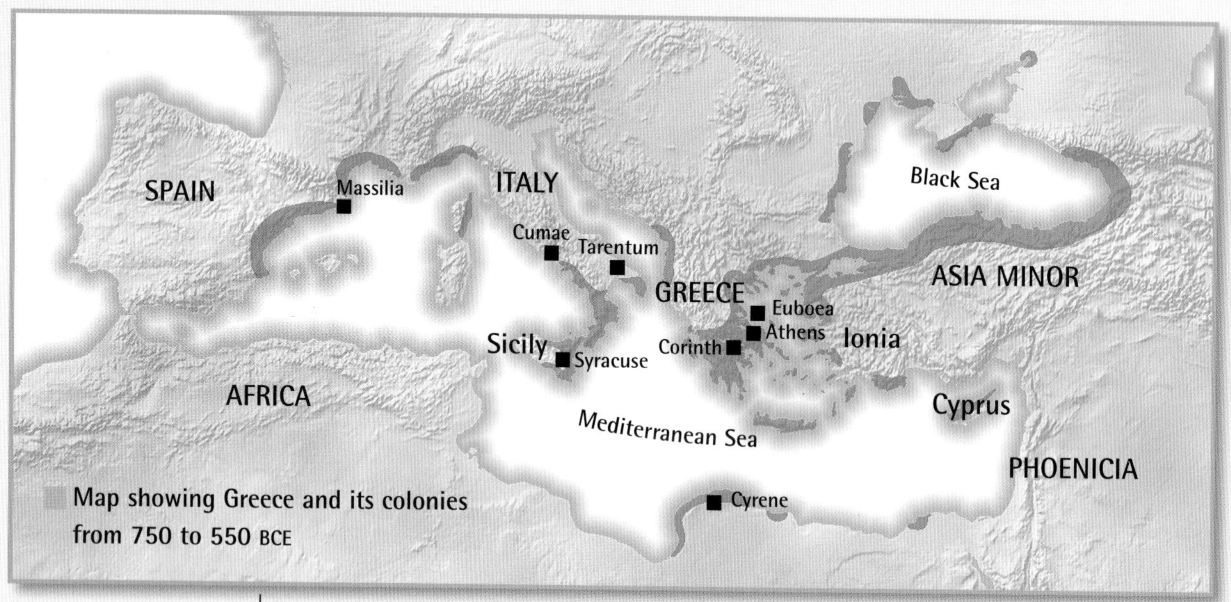

Map showing Greece and its colonies from 750 to 550 BCE

OVERSEAS SETTLEMENT
The Greek world expanded rapidly as citizens left their homes to start new settlements overseas. Settlers were accepted as fully Greek and had the same rights as Greeks on the mainland. Founding a colony was often a dangerous process. First, there was a long sea voyage, followed by the threat of attack on landing.

It is in this period that the Greek city-states began to emerge. Each city-state was called a *polis* (from which we get our word politics). The polis comprised a city, together with the agricultural land and farming villages of the surrounding area. All citizens had free and open access to law and justice. Women and slaves, however, were not counted as citizens. As time went on, many city-states started to introduce their own coinage and systems of measurement. They cherished their independence and they had good reason to be self-confident. The polis as an institution lasted for some eight centuries.

TEMPLE OF CONCORD
The Greek city-states of Sicily and southern Italy grew to be among the wealthiest in the Greek world, flourishing on the trade of tin and silver. This photograph shows the Temple of Concord at Agrigento in Sicily.

As the Greeks moved out of the Dark Age, it seems that they were filled with dynamic energy and purpose. In this period, groups of citizens sailed across the Mediterranean to start new colonies in southern Italy and Sicily. It may be that some settlers wanted land, but it is also likely that many Greeks travelled to Italy in order to exploit the region's rich supplies of metals. New markets opened up, and new trading links were developed. But colonization and immigration were not confined to Italy and Sicily. From the 8th to the 6th centuries BCE, the Greeks travelled wherever their ships could take them – to escape hunger, to seek fortune and adventure, or to find new lands to rule.

Documents surviving from the end of this period of overseas expansion explain how the operations were planned. New colonies were selected for their natural harbours and good agricultural land. When a city decided to form a settlement elsewhere, it chose a leader to become the founder. One son from each family accompanied his father, and they would be given a portion of land when they arrived. It was such an important undertaking that anyone who refused to sail was put to death and all his property confiscated. There were often strong ties between the Greek cities and their colonies. But there were occasions when disagreements broke out, and in exceptional circumstances, a city-state might even go to war.

TORTOISE COIN
The islanders of Aegina (an island between Athens and southern Greece) were great seafarers and traders. They issued the first Greek coins in about 600 BCE, and stamped a tortoise on them as an identity mark. Other cities chose their own symbols.

LAND OF PLENTY
Grapes and olives were the staple crops of Sicily. The island was very fertile, and the settlers were soon growing wheat to export to other parts of the Greek world.

Merchant ships

As trade flourished, the Black Sea and the Mediterranean were filled with merchant ships carrying honey, perfume, wheat, wine, olives, timber and bales of wool. Copper came from Cyprus, tin from Spain, incense from Arabia, ivory from Africa and slaves from the shores of the Black Sea. The ships that carried these large cargoes were broad and deep-bellied. They had a single square sail, and a steersman sat at the back to steer the ship with an oar fixed to the side. Because storms blew up suddenly in the Mediterranean, sea captains kept close to the shore and rarely braved the dangers of the open sea.

HOMER
According to tradition, Homer came from the island of Chios, and was blind. His epic poems, the *Iliad* and the *Odyssey*, were written down in the 7th century BCE and are still enjoyed today.

Altogether more than 150 Greek settlements were founded, stretching all the way from the eastern end of the Black Sea to the coast of southern France and Spain. Trading posts were established all around the Black Sea and the Mediterranean, creating wealth and prosperity throughout the colonies. Sicily and southern Italy were so densely settled and grew so rich that the area became known as "Greater Greece". In this period of trade and colonization, the Mediterranean must have been criss-crossed with a long procession of ships, spreading the Greek way of life across the known world.

But this period of activity and energy was also a time of looking back. The Greeks regarded the heroes of their past with pride. In the 8th century BCE, the Greek poet Homer began to compose poems that celebrated the exploits of the "heroic age". Epic poems such as the *Iliad* and the *Odyssey* retold stories that had been passed on from generation to generation. These stories had been sung at feasts and celebrations to the music of the lyre or to a wind instrument called the *aulos*. The best-loved stories were those of

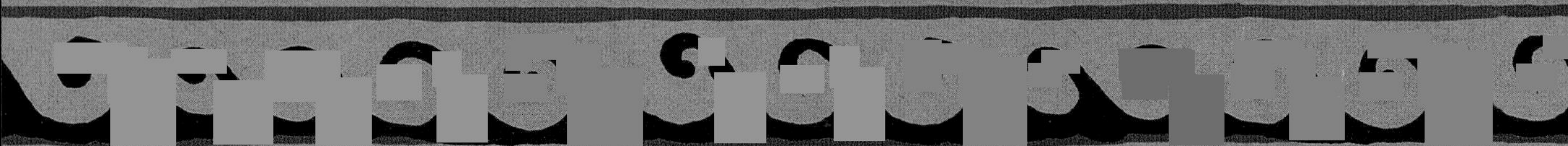

the Trojan War, and around this time, new shrines were built for Homeric heroes such as Achilles and Agamemnon. So the Greeks cherished the memory of the past and kept it alive. It could be said that they had to rediscover their past before they could move confidently into the future.

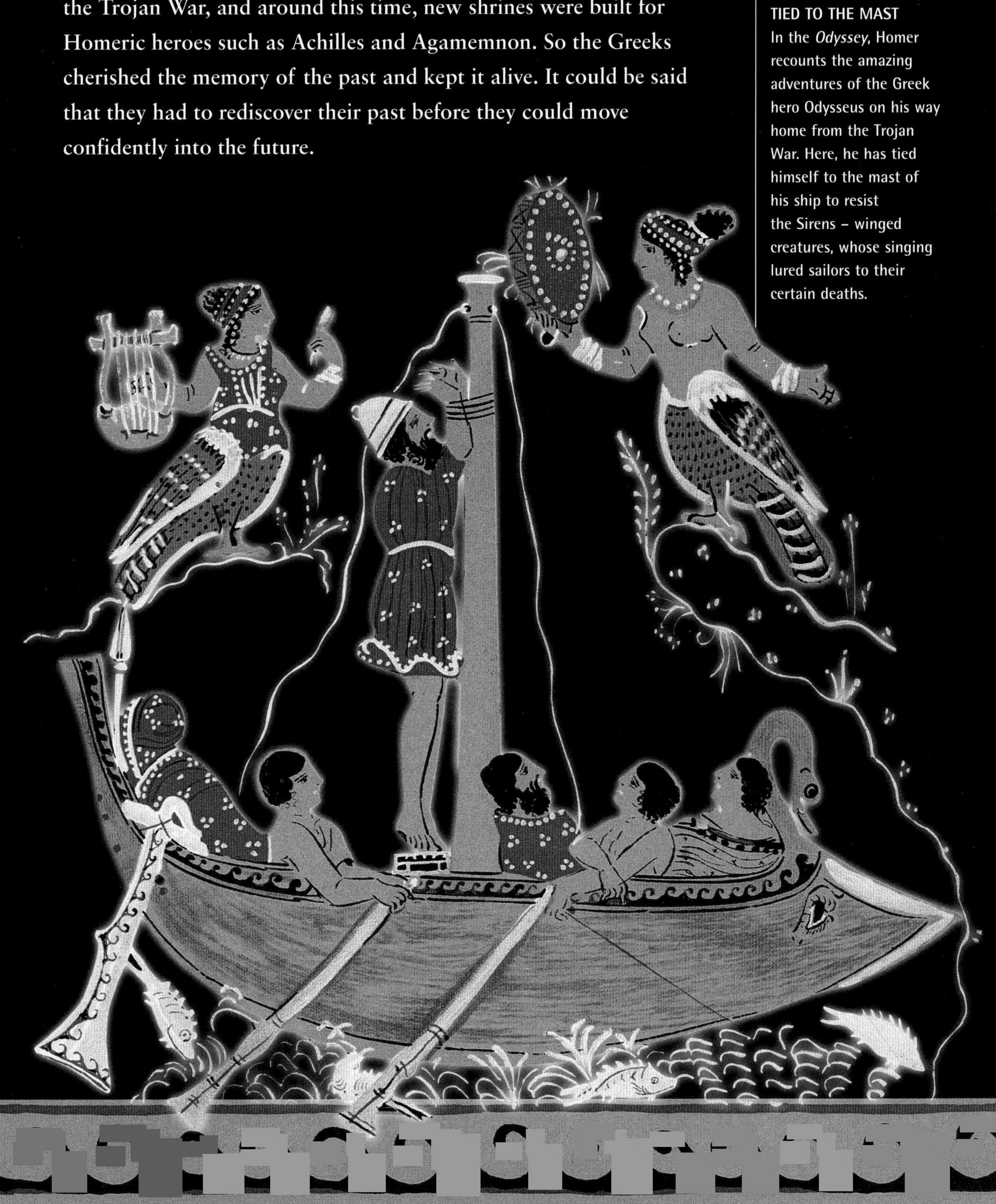

TIED TO THE MAST
In the *Odyssey*, Homer recounts the amazing adventures of the Greek hero Odysseus on his way home from the Trojan War. Here, he has tied himself to the mast of his ship to resist the Sirens – winged creatures, whose singing lured sailors to their certain deaths.

CHAPTER THREE

Gods, heroes *and* tyrants

In the 8th century BCE, there was an astonishing leap forward in Greek culture. Traders took to the seas again, and new forms of art and pottery emerged. Small villages grew into city-states, and there was increasing contact with other lands.

THE NEW ERA OF GREEK REVIVAL, which lasted from 800 to 500 BCE, is known as the Archaic Age. During this period, the population rose and the standard of living improved. New religious festivals and celebrations brought previously isolated communities together, and vases of this period show scenes of dancing and processions. But the most important advance of all was the rediscovery of writing. Once the Greeks had developed an alphabet, they were able to write down the stories and songs that earlier generations had recited from memory. The Greeks did not invent the alphabet, but adopted the system of the Phoenicians – a trading people from the Middle East. They improved the Phoenician system by adding letters to signify vowel sounds. In the process, they created the alphabet that is the ancestor of all European alphabets.

◄ A view of Mount Olympus, home of the gods

EARLY ALPHABET
The text on this plaque uses the Phoenician alphabet and records the building of a shrine. The Phoenicians were traders from the area we now know as the Lebanon.

PENS AND TABLETS
The writing on this pottery fragment is in Greek. The Greek alphabet is the ancestor of our alphabet, and the word itself comes from the Greek letters A and B, alpha and beta.

The rediscovery of writing enabled citizens to keep records, pass on messages and offer dedications to the gods. Archaeologists have found inscriptions on objects such as cups and jugs, which give us a fascinating insight into everyday life in Greece. One inscription on a goblet reads, "I am the cup of Nestor, good to drink from." Another declares that, "this jug will be the prize for the dancer who dances better than all the others." Before the spread of literacy, stories and myths of gods and heroes were passed down by word of mouth from generation to generation. In writing down their stories, Greek poets, such as Homer, created the beginnings of European literature.

The Greeks could not imagine a world without gods. They felt the presence of gods in their local streams and rivers and in their caves and mountains. Each city-state had its own patron god or goddess. Athena, for example, was the patron goddess of Athens, while Artemis was the patron goddess of Ephesus. According to the poets, the 12 most important gods lived at the top of Mount Olympus, the tallest mountain in Greece. These gods were known as the Olympians. From high in the clouds, the gods looked down upon men and women, judging their behaviour and influencing their lives from above. The Greeks believed the gods could take on human form and visit the earth. Sometimes they fell in love with humans and even had children with them. Some gods took a dislike to certain mortals, or to certain cities, and did their best to destroy them. Zeus, king of the

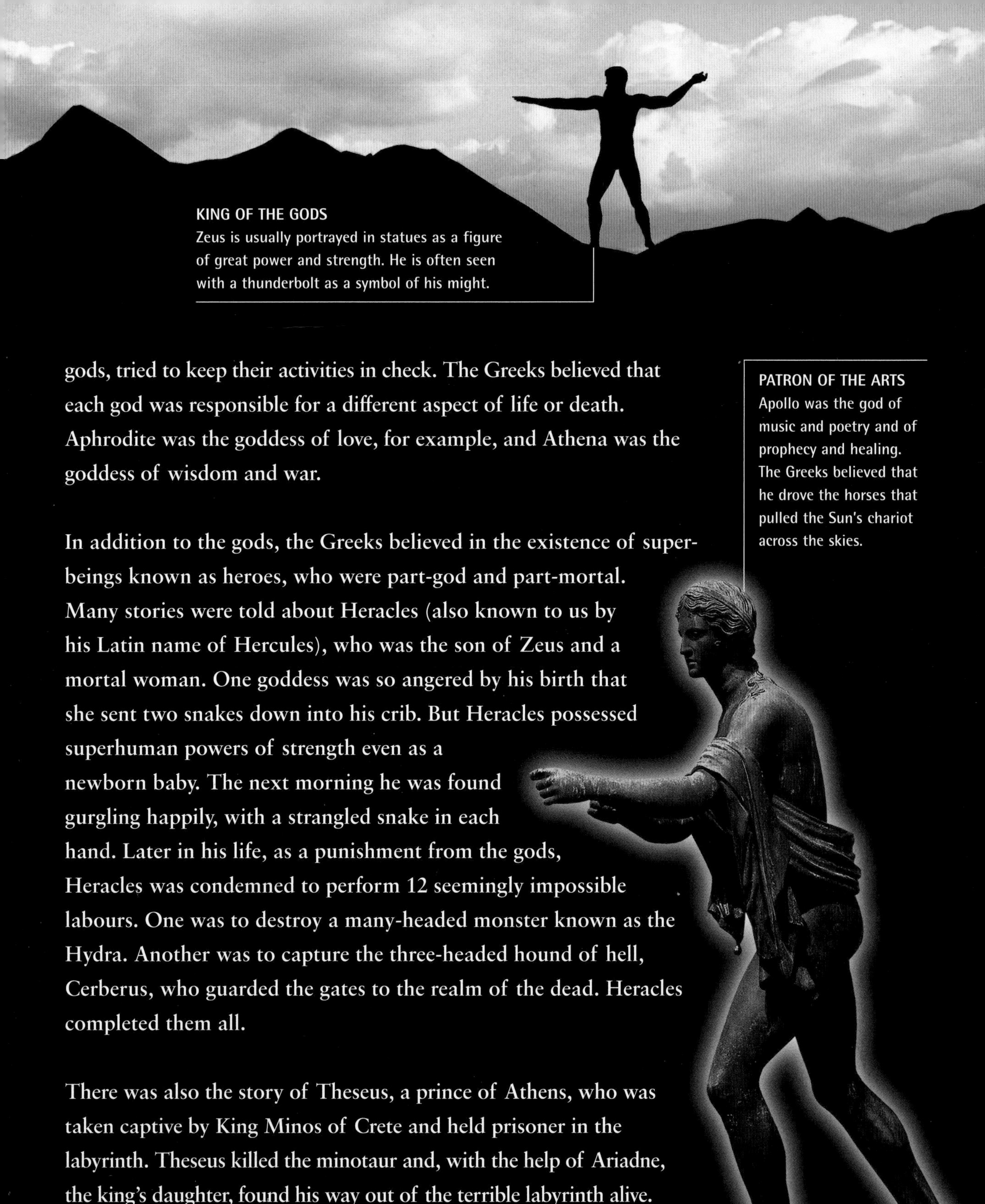

KING OF THE GODS
Zeus is usually portrayed in statues as a figure of great power and strength. He is often seen with a thunderbolt as a symbol of his might.

gods, tried to keep their activities in check. The Greeks believed that each god was responsible for a different aspect of life or death. Aphrodite was the goddess of love, for example, and Athena was the goddess of wisdom and war.

PATRON OF THE ARTS
Apollo was the god of music and poetry and of prophecy and healing. The Greeks believed that he drove the horses that pulled the Sun's chariot across the skies.

In addition to the gods, the Greeks believed in the existence of super-beings known as heroes, who were part-god and part-mortal. Many stories were told about Heracles (also known to us by his Latin name of Hercules), who was the son of Zeus and a mortal woman. One goddess was so angered by his birth that she sent two snakes down into his crib. But Heracles possessed superhuman powers of strength even as a newborn baby. The next morning he was found gurgling happily, with a strangled snake in each hand. Later in his life, as a punishment from the gods, Heracles was condemned to perform 12 seemingly impossible labours. One was to destroy a many-headed monster known as the Hydra. Another was to capture the three-headed hound of hell, Cerberus, who guarded the gates to the realm of the dead. Heracles completed them all.

There was also the story of Theseus, a prince of Athens, who was taken captive by King Minos of Crete and held prisoner in the labyrinth. Theseus killed the minotaur and, with the help of Ariadne, the king's daughter, found his way out of the terrible labyrinth alive.

THE CRETAN BULL
Heracles' seventh labour was to capture the wild bull of Crete, shown here on a vase painting. The "honeysuckle" decoration running around the top of the vase was a popular pattern in Greek art.

Poets were fascinated by the story of Jason who sailed in quest of a golden fleece, which was guarded by a fierce dragon, and by the story of Narcissus, who was so beautiful that he fell in love with his own image reflected in the water of a pond. He lingered on the bank, gazing down at himself, not eating or drinking, until he died.

Rituals and ceremonies played an important part in Greek culture. There was one very strange ritual in Greek society, known as "scapegoating". One person was chosen to take on the ills of a community – he was said to be cursed and was thrown out of the city in the hope that disaster would be averted. For a whole year before this event took place, the chosen scapegoat was treated very well, and when the year ended, he was treated to a lavish dinner. Then, to the sound of flutes, his fellow citizens led him in procession to the city's boundary, and he was chased out of the city with sticks and stones. The citizens then marched back into the city without once looking back.

BALANCING ACT
In the course of his eleventh labour, Heracles had to support the heavens on his shoulders. This 19th-century statue shows Heracles wearing his famous lionskin as a cloak.

The ritual was very old and may have been connected with an ancient magic cult. Archaeologists have found charms and magical dolls with the names of victims written upon them, which may have been related to scapegoating.

WARRIOR WOMEN
The Greeks were fascinated by the myth of the Amazons, who were a fierce tribe of women warriors. This tomb painting shows two Amazon warriors attacking a Greek soldier.

There were also a great many religious ceremonies aimed at pleasing the gods and gaining their help. Many of these ceremonies took place outdoors and involved feasting, singing and dancing. At some festivals, children were pushed on swings above sacred drinking vessels. At others, they carried around branches of olive trees, decorated with fruit and pieces of wool. At the centre of these festivals was an animal sacrifice in which an ox, sheep, pig or goat was slaughtered upon an altar. The animal's blood was offered to the god, while its flesh was cooked and eaten by the worshippers.

All the most important activities in Greek society – games, theatrical events and celebrations – were dedicated to a particular god or goddess. The Olympic Games, for example, were part of a festival dedicated to the god Zeus. These were pan-Hellenic (all-Greek) games, which meant that athletes from all over Greece were allowed to take part. Some centuries later, a Greek historian calculated that the Olympic Games first took place in 776 BCE. The Greeks used this date to mark the beginning of their true history.

The Olympic Games were held every four years at the sanctuary of Zeus at Olympia, in western Greece. The games attracted athletes and spectators from all over the Greek world. Before the

DRAGON'S MEAT
When Jason tried to seize the golden fleece, he was swallowed by the dragon guarding it. The goddess Athena, seen here with her owl, stepped in to save him.

SACRED PLACES
This sanctuary, dedicated to Athena, is at Delphi on the slopes of Mount Parnassus, believed to be a favourite haunt of the gods. Sanctuaries were often in remote places like mountain tops or caves. They were sacred enclosures containing an altar that stood in front of the temple.

games started, oxen were sacrificed at the altar of Zeus in the centre of the sanctuary enclosure. If wars were being fought at the time, everyone would stop fighting and observe a truce so that the competitors could travel to and from Olympia in safety. The Olympic Games took place for more than 1,000 years until the Roman emperor Theodosius abolished them in 393 CE. During their long history, the games became an important symbol of Greek identity and Greek culture. The modern Olympic Games were revived in 1890 in imitation of the original games.

The competitions took place over a period of five days. The highest honour of the games was to win the short sprint known as the *stadion* (from which we get the word stadium), which was the oldest of the contests held at Olympia. One of the most challenging events was the Pentathlon, which was designed to find the best athlete. The Pentathlon consisted of five events – discus throwing, javelin throwing, jumping, running and wrestling. The opening event at the Olympic Games was the chariot race. This was an ancient sport going back to

SONG AND DANCE
Paintings of festivals and feasts often decorated Greek pottery of this time. This painted border on a wine bowl shows a procession of people celebrating a festival.

the Bronze Age, when Greek warriors still used chariots to ride into battle. The race was extremely dangerous. The jockeys rode bareback (without any saddles) and accidents were common. Four-horse chariot races were held in an arena called the hippodrome (*hippos* is the Greek word for horse). One of the most popular events was a dangerous sport called *pankration*, which seems to have been a mixture of boxing and wrestling and could last for hours. A contestant was allowed to use any tactic apart from biting and eye-gouging to overcome his opponent. Curiously enough, for a people who lived so close to the sea, there were no swimming competitions.

HOPLITE RACE
One particular race at Olympia was for Greek foot soldiers, called hoplites. They had to run a distance of 400 m (440 yd) wearing their full body armour of helmet, breastplate and greaves (leg protectors). Later, the race became less tough – the runners only had to wear a helmet and carry a shield.

Usually, the contestants in the Olympic Games were naked. The word *gymnos* (meaning naked in Greek) is the root of our word gymnasium. In Greece, the gymnasium was the place where all the boys and men of the city went to train and exercise. Women were not allowed to take part in the

The Olympic site

The Olympic Games were held over a period of five days at the sanctuary of Zeus at Olympia. The altar and temple of Zeus originally lay within a sacred grove of trees beside a river, but as the athletic festival gained importance, more buildings were built outside the sanctuary enclosure. Every four years, Olympia swarmed with up to 40,000 visitors for the duration of the festival. There were temples and treasuries, a banqueting room, a guest house and a *palaistra* (sports ground) for wrestling and boxing. The great temple of Zeus, built in the 5th century BCE, contained a colossal gold and ivory statue of the god by the sculptor Phidias, whose workshop has been excavated at the site.

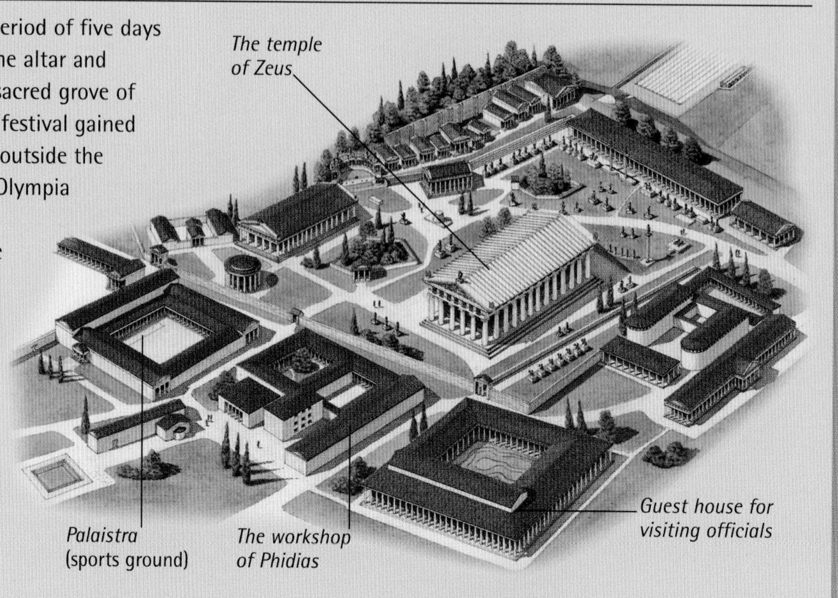

VICTOR'S CROWN
The sacred olive tree, from which the winners' wreaths were made, stood behind the temple of Zeus at Olympia. A herald announced the name of the winner after each event, but the prizes were not awarded until the last day of the games.

Olympic Games (although they were allowed to enter teams of horses in the chariot races). Any married woman discovered at the Olympic Games was put to death by being thrown off a nearby mountain.

The winners did not receive money or silver cups, but a simple wreath of wild olive leaves. In the pursuit of excellence, that was considered reward enough. Yet victory brought enormous prestige and fame. Although the contestants competed as individuals (not as representatives of their cities), successful athletes were celebrated as heroes in their home cities and were given great honours on their return. In Athens, for example, Olympic victors were offered free meals for life. Others had statues put up in their honour or had poems written about their achievements. So great were the influence and popularity of the Olympics that athletic contests started to spring up all over Greece, attended by thousands of athletes and spectators.

In the 8th century BCE, each city-state had its own sanctuary dedicated to the city's patron god or goddess. However, some major sanctuaries came to be held sacred by all Greeks and were known as pan-Hellenic sanctuaries. One such site was the sanctuary of Apollo at Delphi, which nestled on the slopes of Mount Parnassus in central Greece. Apollo was one of the most influential of the Greek gods, and his sanctuary at Delphi was the site of a famous oracle. The Greeks thought that gods could give them practical advice in the form of oracles – forecasts and advice from priests or priestesses who acted as mouthpieces for the gods. People would travel to Delphi (and to oracles at other sites) from all over Greece to ask questions about the future. For example, before a city-state went to war, its rulers might ask Apollo if their enterprise would be successful. Individuals also asked questions about personal affairs, such as forthcoming marriages or success in business.

Before a question was put to the god, a goat would be sacrificed on the sacred altar. First, the goat was sprinkled with cold water. If it shivered, it meant that Apollo was ready to answer. His answers were conveyed through a priestess known as the Pythia, who sat on a three-legged stool before a golden statue of the god. Here, she would fall into a

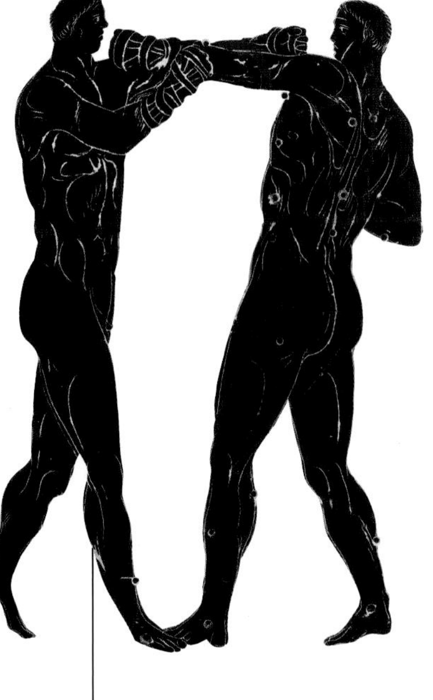

OLYMPIC BOXING
Boxing was a favourite sport of the Greeks. Instead of boxing gloves, fighters wrapped strips of leather around their fists for protection.

SPORTING SCENES
Pictures of athletes often decorated vases. From left to right, an athlete chooses a discus, a long-jumper lifts heavy stones called *halteres* (with which he had to jump) and wrestlers try to throw each other off balance.

FAMOUS CHAMPION
Theogenes was a famous athlete who was reputed to have won more than 1,400 boxing contests. He boxed for 22 years and was never once defeated. This altar at Olympia was dedicated to his memory.

trance and give answers to the questions. Sometimes a foolish or unwise questioner might misunderstand her responses. For example, Croesus, a king of Lydia in Asia Minor, asked the oracle whether or not he should attack the Persian empire. He was told that if he went to war, a great kingdom would be destroyed. Certain of victory, Croesus began his campaign against the Persians. But he had misinterpreted the answer. It was his own kingdom that was about to be destroyed.

No one ever really doubted the truth of Apollo's messages, and the tradition of the oracle seems to have been very profitable for the guardians of the shrine, who charged for their services. Delphi became one of the most important religious centres of Greek society, and for many centuries, it exerted an enormous influence on decisions of life or death, peace or war. The Greeks would often consult a wide range of oracles to foretell the future. The oracle at Dodona in northern Greece, took the form of an oak tree, and people were instructed to listen to the

SACRED TO APOLLO
These stone pillars have been re-erected from fallen columns on the site of the sanctuary at Apollo that housed the Oracle at Delphi. In ancient times, travel to this remote mountain site must have been very hard, yet people came from all over Greece to consult the oracle.

FABULOUSLY RICH
Croesus, the last king of Lydia, was famed for his wealth, and his name has become associated with great riches. This 17th-century painting depicts him in the costume of a monarch of the day, showing off his fabulous treasures of gold.

voice of the mighty god Zeus rustling in the leaves. Other sanctuaries in Greece were thought to have special powers of healing. Pilgrims visiting these sanctuaries would fall asleep in the hope that the god would send a dream to cure them while they slept. Sometimes, sick or injured people would leave clay models of their damaged limbs as an offering of thanks.

Sanctuaries stood within an area known as a sacred precinct. Anything within this area belonged to the god or goddess and was under his or her protection. So, in theory, exiles and criminals could stay within the sanctuary without fear of capture. Some city-states placed their treasuries in sanctuaries, in the knowledge that they would not be robbed. The city-state of Athens, for example, kept valuables of gold and silver in the sanctuary at Delphi.

Worshippers who could not afford to sacrifice animals or offer valuable objects might leave smaller gifts, such as figurines, pins or vases. Some Greeks liked to dedicate artefacts called tripods to the gods. A tripod was a three-legged vessel of bronze, gold or silver, decorated with engravings. In the 8th century, tripods were not only dedicated as offerings to the gods, but were also awarded as prizes in various sporting competitions. Archaeologists have found a series of bronze tripods at the site of Olympia, which were thought to have been prizes in the early days of the competition.

TOKEN OF THANKS
This marble carving of a leg was hung in the sanctuary of Asclepius (the god of healing) as a thank-you offering.

By the 7th century BCE, the Greeks were becoming wealthy on trade. The cargoes exported on Greek ships included pots of perfume and ointment as well as great jars filled with wine and olive oil. Other exports included pottery and leather goods as well as building materials such as marble. In turn, the Greek cities imported grain and much-needed metals, such as copper and iron. There was also a thriving trade in slaves, who made up a large part of the Greek workforce.

DISTANT TRADE
This bronze vessel, known as a *krater*, was used to mix water and wine. The Greeks traded many beautiful objects like this, and a fine bronze *krater* has been found as far away as central France.

As trade flourished, the city-states continued to develop and to expand. Each city-state was governed by a group of wealthy aristocrats. These ruling groups were known as oligarchies, which means "the rule of the few". Conflict often arose between the aristocrats and the ordinary citizens. In the Greek city of Mytilene, the aristocratic leaders armed themselves with clubs and went round beating any citizen they disliked. In some city-states, people were ruled by individual leaders called tyrants. To us, the word tyrant suggests

DOLPHIN POT
Olive trees grow abundantly in Greece, and olive oil was exported all round the Mediterranean. This dolphin skimming over the waves decorates a small container that once held household olive oil.

cruelty and injustice, but to the Greeks the word simply meant a single ruler. The tyrants were usually aristocrats who gained power by winning the support of less well-off citizens. Some were war-heroes or clever politicians who promised an end to the exploitation of small farmers by rich landowners. Others promised to end damaging feuds that divided a particular town or city. Many tyrants were good leaders who helped to improve their cities by introducing reforms or by encouraging new architecture.

Tyrants on the whole did not last long. They had become the leaders of the people by taking up popular causes, but the people could just as easily turn against them. Many tyrannies only survived for the lifetime of the individual leader, although some tyrant families managed to hold on to power for two or three generations. In some cities, the tyrants were succeeded by new aristocrats, but in others there was a move towards a radical new system of government called a democracy, or the rule of the people.

The history of Greece in the next two centuries is best understood by looking at two very different city-states in terms of character, history and systems of government. The bitter and turbulent wars they fought against each other ultimately helped to weaken the power of Greece. Those two city-states are Sparta and Athens – the two greatest forces in Greek history.

WISE TYRANT
Pittacus of Mytilene was a philosopher who was made tyrant in 589 BCE to protect his city from a group of exiled aristocrats. Famous for his wisdom, he gave up power after ten years.

CHAPTER FOUR

The power *of* Sparta

The strange and frightening city-state of Sparta lay in the south of the Peloponnese, the peninsula that forms the southern half of the Greek mainland. It was a fierce and brutal society that was determined to keep its neighbours in a constant state of fear.

SPARTA LAY IN A WIDE RIVER valley, cut off by mountains on either side. The remoteness of the landscape was an advantage to the warring Spartans, with the high mountains surrounding it forming a natural defence. It was founded in the 10th century BCE by a group of people called the Dorians, who had defeated the original inhabitants of the area. The state of Sparta was formed from the union of five neighbouring villages, and throughout its history it retained its village-like appearance. But the territory of Sparta was very large, covering an area of some 7,700 sq km (3,000 sq miles). The Spartans had very simple houses and no great public buildings. The Spartan mind and imagination were occupied only with matters of war and domination. All men had to serve in the army, and their whole lives were dedicated to learning the art of battle.

◀ Detail of a vase from Sparta, showing warriors in combat

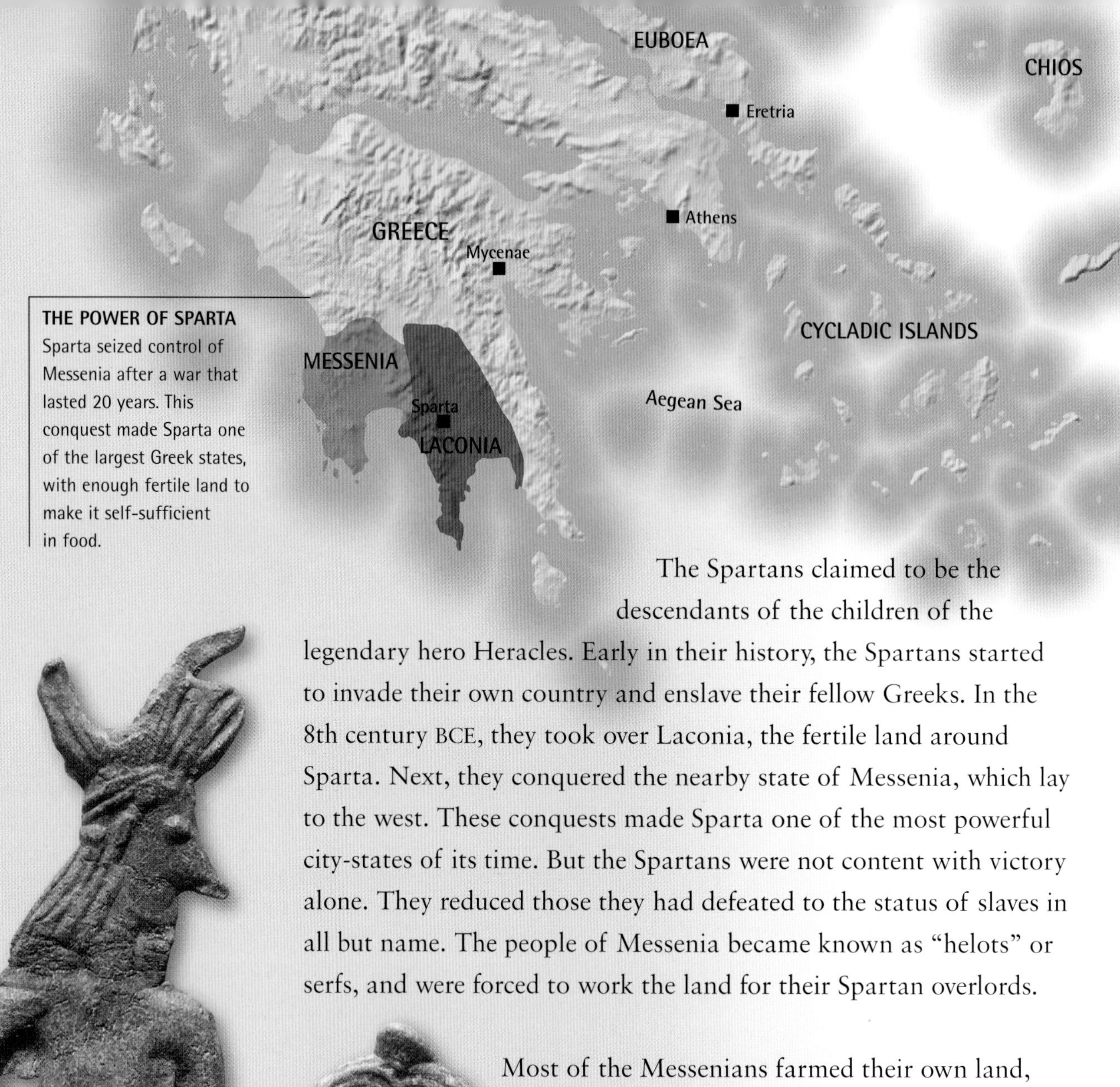

THE POWER OF SPARTA
Sparta seized control of Messenia after a war that lasted 20 years. This conquest made Sparta one of the largest Greek states, with enough fertile land to make it self-sufficient in food.

The Spartans claimed to be the descendants of the children of the legendary hero Heracles. Early in their history, the Spartans started to invade their own country and enslave their fellow Greeks. In the 8th century BCE, they took over Laconia, the fertile land around Sparta. Next, they conquered the nearby state of Messenia, which lay to the west. These conquests made Sparta one of the most powerful city-states of its time. But the Spartans were not content with victory alone. They reduced those they had defeated to the status of slaves in all but name. The people of Messenia became known as "helots" or serfs, and were forced to work the land for their Spartan overlords.

Most of the Messenians farmed their own land, but they were obliged to give half of their produce to their Spartan masters. As a mark of their inferiority, the helots were forced to wear animal skins and caps made of dog-skin. Every year they were given a ritual beating. If any helots tried to run away, they would be pursued by professional "slave-catchers" and killed. The helots

SANCTUARY OFFERINGS
These tiny figurines, one of the goddess Artemis, the other of a soldier, were among thousands of offerings left at the sanctuary to Artemis that stood beside the River Eurotas in Sparta.

YOUNG SPARTANS
This painting by 19th-century French artist Edgar Degas shows Spartan boys and girls exercising together. Sparta was unique among Greek city-states in teaching girls athletics.

were kept in slavery for 300 years and, although they sometimes tried to rebel, they could never overcome the might and efficiency of their hated Spartan overlords. This is all the more remarkable since the helots outnumbered the Spartans by about seven to one.

The descendants of the people who had been defeated by the Spartans were classed as either helots or *perioikoi*, which means "those who dwell around". Most of the defeated Laconians were known as *perioikoi*. Although they were not classed as Spartan citizens, they were free and were allowed to trade and govern themselves. In return for their freedom, they had to serve in the Spartan army and follow wherever the Spartans led. Only men who were born in the city of Sparta were regarded as citizens.

The constant risk of a helot revolt turned Sparta into a military state. The Spartan way of life was designed to raise men who would be able

CITY OF THE PLAIN
Sparta stood in the middle of a fertile river plain surrounded by rugged mountains, which gave it natural protection from its enemies. The setting remains little changed today, but the ruins of ancient Sparta are mostly buried beneath the modern town.

DONKEY DRINKING CUP
Spartan boys were made to watch helots drinking large quantities of undiluted wine to show them the effects of excess alcohol. This drinking cup delivers the same message in a humorous fashion.

to keep the helots under control. When a Spartan male child was born, he was examined by a council of elders. If he was thought too weak or too deformed to be of use to the state, he was abandoned and left to die on a neighbouring mountain. At the age of seven, Spartan boys were taken away from their families to be educated by the state. They lived in barracks and were organized into "packs". Life in the barracks was brutal, and the boys were trained to endure pain and punishment. Once a year, Spartan boys were taken to the sanctuary of Artemis on the banks of the River Eurotas, where they would be flogged as a demonstration of their toughness and endurance. All boys were made to go barefoot, and their hair was cut short. To make them self-reliant, they were given very little to eat and were encouraged to steal food. If a boy was caught, he was severely beaten, not for stealing but for being found out. There is the famous story of a Spartan boy who stole a fox and hid it under his cloak. When the fox began to tear at the boy, he allowed the creature to rip out his guts, rather than cry out and be discovered. The boy died in agony.

SPARTAN DELICACY
The Spartan speciality was a black soup made out of salt, blood and vinegar. No one in the rest of Greece would drink it.

At the age of 20, young Spartans left one form of communal life to join another. Adult Spartan men were full-time warriors, who lived in barracks and ate, drank and exercised together. Their communal meal was held in the evenings, and they had to make their way there in the dark – no torches were allowed to light the route. It was a way of training their warriors to attack and survive in the dark. Before he became a citizen, every young Spartan had to go through a rite of passage. He was sent out into the countryside at night, armed with only a dagger, and told to kill any helot he came across. It was a form of licensed murder. Spartan soldiers were not permitted to marry until they reached the age of 30, and even then they were not allowed to live with their wives and families. All soldiers were given land by the state and helots to farm it. This meant they could devote themselves entirely to the army.

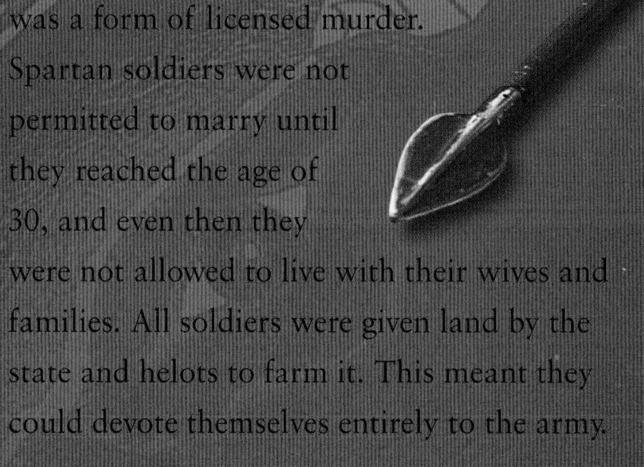

Sparta was a society of soldiers in a state of perpetual warfare. When they joined the barracks, young men were ordered to grow their hair long and to grow a long beard (although they were forbidden to grow moustaches). This was to give them a fierce and warlike appearance. The Greek historian Herodotus recorded that Spartan soldiers always carried out the ritual of combing their long hair when they felt they were about to put their lives at risk.

As a result of this training, the Spartans created the most efficient army in the whole of Greece. All Spartan citizens had to keep themselves fit at all times as they were liable to be called up for military service until the age of 60. Spartan warriors were well known for their courage and their discipline, based on a profound

PERPETUAL WARFARE
Foot soldiers were called hoplites after the hoplon, the large heavy shield they carried. They charged towards the enemy in tight ranks, holding their shields in front of them, and using their spears as jabbing weapons.

SPARTAN CURRENCY
Until the end of the 5th century BCE, the Spartans did not use silver currency. On some occasions, they used iron cooking spits like these instead of coins.

TRADING SCENE
This bowl is a rare example of Spartan pottery. Made in about 560 BCE, it shows a lively trading scene in the Greek colony of Cyrene in North Africa. Until the 6th century BCE, the Spartans were active traders with other Greek colonies. After that time, the Spartans had little contact with the outside world, and trade began to die out.

sense of duty to their state. They were trained to withstand hunger and pain and were taught how to attack ferociously. All soldiers were dressed in red, so that bloodstains from their wounds would not be visible. One Spartan poet told the young men of the Spartan army that, during battle, they should not reflect on the greatness or importance of life. The protection of the state was more important away in battle would be despised by everyone, and lose all his rights.

Because its army was hardly ever beaten in battle, Sparta never built defensive walls to protect itself from invaders. Its rulers were supremely confident that they could resist any attack, even though they were surrounded by enemies. Their only real fear was that the helots they had enslaved would rise up in revolt against them. The Spartans had no luxuries, but prided themselves on their brute strength, courage and determination. Their tough, disciplined existence would prepare them to deal with any helot uprising.

Spartan women seem to have had more freedom than women in other Greek cities. Young girls were educated from the age of seven. Like their brothers, they lived, slept and trained in barracks. They learned to read and write but, most importantly, they were trained from an early age in athletics, gymnastics and combat sports. At the age of 18, if a Spartan girl passed her fitness test, she was assigned a husband and allowed to return home. Spartan girls were regarded as the future mothers of a warrior breed. They were expected to keep fit so that they would give birth to healthy sons who would grow up to be good soldiers.

READY FOR BATTLE
Wrapped in his military cloak, with his long locks of hair falling over his shoulders, this Spartan warrior wears a characteristic grim and fierce expression.

INDEPENDENT WOMEN
Wearing a very short skirt, a Spartan girl competes in a running race. This scandalized the Athenians who did not let women take part in sporting events.

A WISE MAN
Chilon, an *ephor* (ruler) of Sparta in the 6th century BCE, was one of the "Seven Wise Men of Greece" who won fame for their wise sayings. He is said to have died of joy on hearing that his son had won an Olympic wreath.

Spartan women were much more independent than the women of other Greek city-states. They were allowed to own land and property and they did not have to stay within their houses as the helots did all the housework for them. Much to the disgust of other Greeks, who believed that women should be kept hidden from view, Spartan women sang and danced in front of men. They were also well known for being brave and outspoken. In fact, they were sometimes more ferocious than the men. When one mother saw her son returning alive from a battle in which everyone else had died, she felt such shame that she picked up a rock and killed him.

The state of Sparta had an unusual system of government. It was governed by two kings who ruled together equally. There was also a committee of five men, known as the *ephors*, whose duty it was to keep a watch on the activities of the kings and to make sure that they obeyed their oaths of office. The kings were members of a council of 30 men, who were known as the elders (all the other members had to be over 60 years old). The council of elders acted as a supreme court of justice – they drew up the laws and acted as judges. The council's proposals had to be approved by an assembly made up of Spartan warriors, which met once a month at the time of the full moon. The assembly could only vote for or against measures by shouting "yes"

DUTIES OF A KING
This portrait is of Archidamos III, a king of Sparta in the 4th century BCE. The philosopher Aristotle described the Spartan kings as hereditary generals, as their main duties were to declare war and lead the army in battle.

or "no". The group that shouted the loudest won. The Spartans were very proud of their system and fought fiercely to uphold it. It was a very conservative system of government, but it was one that endured for hundreds of years without significant change. In that sense, perhaps, it can be considered a success.

In the middle of the 6th century BCE, Sparta dominated most of the Peloponnese. They had become the strongest military power in Greece. However, the population of Sparta was steadily declining and the number of soldiers in the army decreased. This was partly because of deaths in battle and partly because wealth in Sparta belonged to fewer and fewer families. Inevitably other citizens became poorer. They could no longer afford to pay their contributions to the army, and so they lost their rights as citizens. To solve this problem, Sparta made a series of alliances with nearby states in the Peloponnese. This alliance was collectively known as the Peloponnesian League. Although the allied cities remained independent, they pledged to give military help when needed under the leadership of Sparta. By the end of the century, Sparta was ready to strike out into central Greece against its most bitter rival – the city-state of Athens.

FALLEN WARRIOR
For Spartans, there was no nobler fate than to die on the battlefield. But in the end, the Spartan state collapsed because it no longer had enough soldiers to fight in its armies.

CHAPTER FIVE

Athens, *master of law*

Athens was the largest and most powerful of the Greek city-states. It was also the centre of Greek culture, famous for its art, drama, history and philosophy. At the heart of the city, stood the great rock of Athens – the Acropolis.

ATHENS WAS SITUATED in a densely populated region called Attica in central Greece. The Athenians lived on the land beneath a hill called the Acropolis. In early times, the Acropolis, meaning "high city", was a fortified citadel, where inhabitants took refuge when the city was under attack from hostile neighbours. Later, it became the most sacred part of the town, where many important temples and sanctuaries were built. Like many other city-states, Athens was ruled by a group of rich aristocrats, who elected nine magistrates called *archons* to manage the affairs of the city. In the 7th-century BCE, the power of the aristocracy in Athens was threatened by the emergence of new rulers called tyrants who wanted to take power for themselves. In about 632 BCE, an Athenian nobleman called Cylon attempted to set up a tyranny in Athens.

◀ A relief-sculpture of a woman playing the lyre

He had been a celebrated victor at the Olympic Games and, like some other successful athletes, decided that he deserved political power. But Cylon was rejected by the Athenian people, and his attempted coup was unsuccessful. Fearing for his life, he claimed sanctuary by the sacred altar of Athena on the Acropolis. Despite promises that he would not be killed, he and his supporters were murdered at the site.

SOLON, THE LAWMAKER
Later generations regarded Solon as the father of Athenian democracy. He was a poet as well as a statesman. "Many rich men are bad," he wrote in one of his poems, "and many good men are poor."

A few years later, the Athenians appointed a severe ruler called Draco (his name means "snake" in Greek). He drew up Athens' first written code of laws which, among other things, made murder a crime. So harsh were the penalties imposed by Draco, it was said that his laws were written in blood rather than in ink. Even today, a particularly tough law or ruling may be described as "draconian".

In 594 BCE, an aristocrat named Solon was appointed *archon*. A wise and just ruler, Solon tried to reform the state and set Athens on the path to democracy. His main aim was to get rid of injustice in public life and establish good order among the people.

He gave food to the poor, cancelled the debts of poverty-stricken farmers and devised a constitution (a system of government) that made wealth, not birth, the qualification for public office. He also abolished slavery as a punishment for getting into debt, and created a system of justice that allowed all citizens accused of a crime to appeal to a court of justice.

After Solon had set out his reforms, he left Athens for ten years, explaining that he was tired of being asked to make improvements to his new constitution. He complained that he had wished to please everyone but, as a result, he had managed to please no one. Nevertheless, he was considered to be one of the first liberators of Athens, the father-figure of a society that would become the most democratic in the world. His laws were so respected that they were displayed on wooden pillars in the Athenian market place. It was he, more than anyone else, who helped to create the class of small farmers and landowners who would play such a crucial part in Athenian society over the centuries that followed.

But, in the 6th century BCE, the emerging democracy of Athens was threatened by squabbling among the aristocratic

GUILT OR INNOCENCE
Solon said that juries made up of citizens should judge cases in the law courts. Under Solon's rule, juries voted with pebbles or a show of hands, but later they used voting disks.

OLIVE TREES
Solon laid down rules on all kinds of subjects, even stipulating that olive trees should grow only to a height of 3 m (9 ft).

OLIVE FARMING
The painting on this bowl shows women gathering olives in baskets. Solon did much to help the cause of farmers in Athens, and encouraged trade throughout the city.

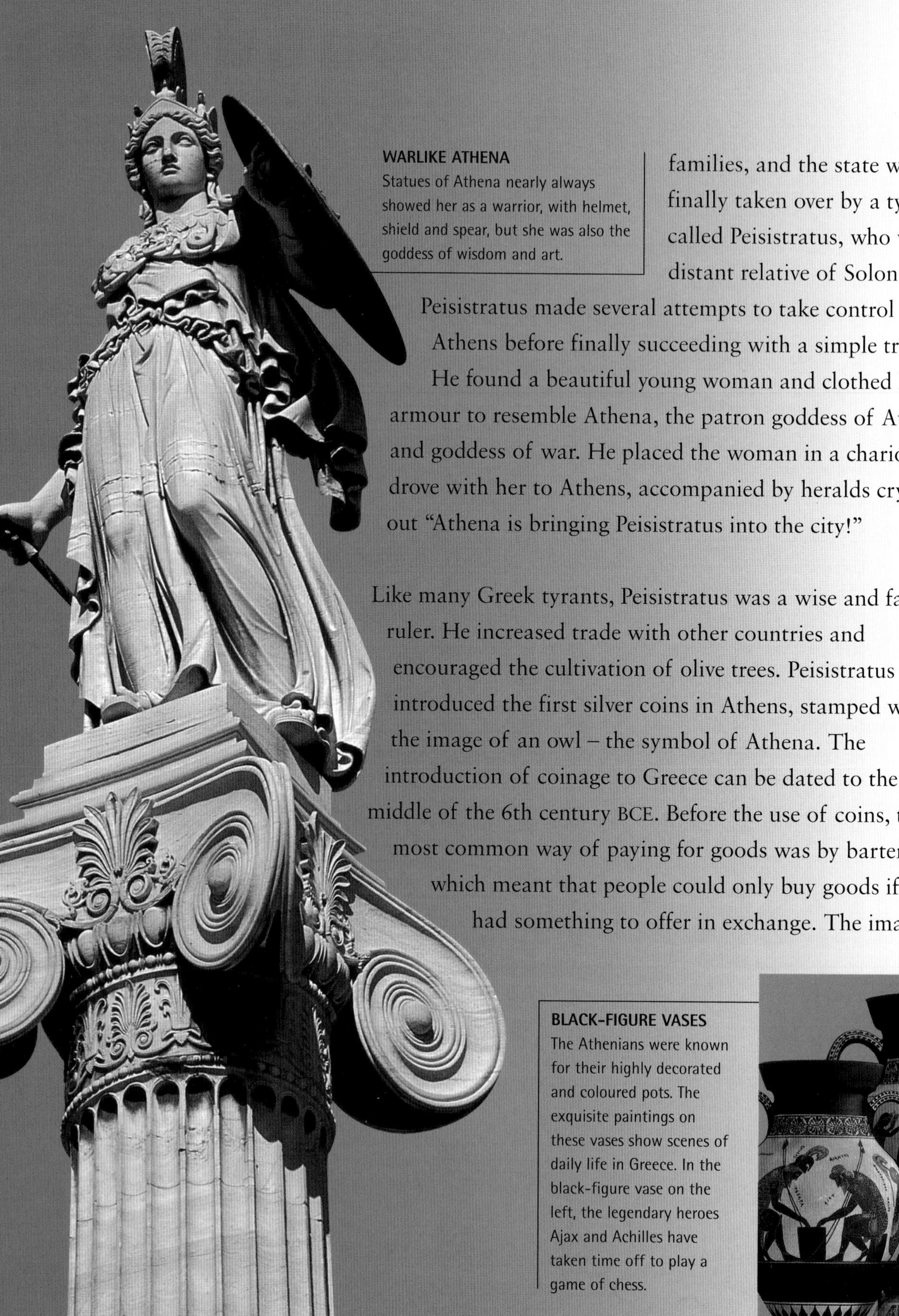

WARLIKE ATHENA
Statues of Athena nearly always showed her as a warrior, with helmet, shield and spear, but she was also the goddess of wisdom and art.

families, and the state was finally taken over by a tyrant called Peisistratus, who was a distant relative of Solon.

Peisistratus made several attempts to take control of Athens before finally succeeding with a simple trick. He found a beautiful young woman and clothed her in armour to resemble Athena, the patron goddess of Athens and goddess of war. He placed the woman in a chariot and drove with her to Athens, accompanied by heralds crying out "Athena is bringing Peisistratus into the city!"

Like many Greek tyrants, Peisistratus was a wise and fair ruler. He increased trade with other countries and encouraged the cultivation of olive trees. Peisistratus also introduced the first silver coins in Athens, stamped with the image of an owl – the symbol of Athena. The introduction of coinage to Greece can be dated to the middle of the 6th century BCE. Before the use of coins, the most common way of paying for goods was by barter, which meant that people could only buy goods if they had something to offer in exchange. The image

BLACK-FIGURE VASES
The Athenians were known for their highly decorated and coloured pots. The exquisite paintings on these vases show scenes of daily life in Greece. In the black-figure vase on the left, the legendary heroes Ajax and Achilles have taken time off to play a game of chess.

BORROWED MONEY
The Greeks did not invent coins, but took the idea from the kingdom of Lydia in Asia Minor, where this hoard was found. The use of coins made trading and the transfer of property easier.

stamped on the coins showed which city-state they were from, and was a way of indicating the financial strength of that area. The first coins were made of lumps of metal called electrum (a mixture of silver and gold), but this was soon changed to silver. Athens was particularly fortunate in having state-owned silver mines at Laurium, in the south of Attica.

Peisistratus began an ambitious programme of public building in Athens. It was a way of giving work to Athenian labourers, and also a way of ensuring that his legacy would be remembered. One of the most important buildings he commissioned was a new temple to Athena on the Acropolis. This spectacular monument was adorned with various sculptures of limestone, together with a band of painted and sculpted decoration known as a frieze.

For the Greeks, the central qualities of both art and architecture were order and symmetry,

Decorated pottery

Greek pots were made in many different shapes, according to their different uses. The best pots of all were made in Athens, where the local clay fired well to a beautiful reddish-brown colour. In the black-figure technique, developed during the time of Peisistratus, black silhouette figures were painted onto the reddish clay background. But soon after 500 BCE, the red-figure technique took over, in which the figures were left unpainted to stand out against a black background.

SYMBOL OF ATHENS
The reverse side of Athenian coins bore the first letters of the city's name, together with an owl, the special bird of the goddess Athena, and an olive branch.

balance and proportion. The purpose of the Greek artist was to give his subjects an aura of calmness and dignity. In early Greek art, painted and sculpted figures had regular, even features, but over time they became more natural-looking and realistic. The Greeks were very interested in the human form and, for the first time, artists and sculptors tried to show human emotion and expression in their work. The most beautiful Greek sculptures of this period were those carved in marble and in bronze. When we see Greek marble statues in museums, they are always white, but at the time they were painted with bright colours such as red and blue.

Under the rule of Peisistratus, Athens flourished and prospered. He undertook great public works and staged spectacular festivals, making Athens the most magnificent city in Greece. As well as building temples on the Acropolis, he planned and erected a large open market and meeting place close to the Acropolis, known as the *agora*, which became the social centre of the city. He also built a gymnasium, where Athenian men could train and exercise, and started a drama competition at the festival dedicated to the god Dionysus. This was to have enormous

HIGH CITY
The Athenians regarded the Acropolis as the most sacred part of their city and adorned it with the marble temples and sanctuaries that dominate the modern city today.

MARKET PLACE
In this painted reconstruction of the market place of Athens, the long colonnaded building on the left is the *stoa*, where the Athenians met every day to talk and to carry out business. Other important buildings included the mint, the law court and the council chamber (*bouleuterion*).

consequences for European literature, because it was from these performances that the first Greek plays developed.

HORSE'S HEAD
Greek sculpted figures gradually became more realistic, showing facial expression and emotion. This marble relief of a horse's head is from one of the pediments of the Parthenon in Athens.

On the death of Peisistratus in 527 BCE, his two sons, Hippias and Hipparchus, took over the government of Athens and ruled for 17 years. They continued their father's building work and turned Athens into a magnificent city of marble. They were both patrons of the arts, and Hipparchus himself introduced the public reading of the poet Homer at Athenian festivals. But the brothers had many enemies among members of the other aristocratic families, and in 514 BCE, Hipparchus was assassinated. Then, one aristocratic family took the drastic step of bribing the priestess of the oracle at Delphi to help them get rid of Hippias by calling in the Spartan army. The Spartans were opposed to tyrant rule, and when they consulted the oracle about their future, she told them to first free Athens from tyranny. So in 510 BCE, the Spartan army marched to Athens and surrounded Hippias, who had taken refuge on the Acropolis. He surrendered and left Athens for ever.

Rivalry between the aristocratic families ended when a reformer named Cleisthenes came to power in 508 BCE. He decided that it was time to introduce political equality within the city-state. He divided the people of Attica into ten new tribes. Each tribe then elected 50 citizens by lot to form a new political council of 500 citizens. This meant that the ordinary citizens of Athens could play a much greater part in public affairs. The men of each tribe also formed separate regiments in the Athenian army, fighting under an elected commander.

DIONYSUS
Peisistratus dedicated his drama competition to Dionysus, the god of wine and patron of the arts. Dionysus was often shown riding a leopard or tiger, with vine leaves in his hair.

Under the system created by Cleisthenes, Attica was divided up into small local areas called *demes* (villages). Citizens were identified by the *deme* from which they came. This helped to break up the power of

HARMODIUS AND ARISTOGEITON
These replica statues are of Harmodius and Aristogeiton, the assassins of the tyrant Hipparchus. They came to be regarded as heroes by later generations.

the family and provided citizens with a sense of belonging. Cleisthenes also gave new powers to the Athenian assembly, which was made up of all the citizens of Athens, and encouraged all citizens to share in the decision-making process. This was an important stage in the development of democracy.

THEMISTOCLES
This coin shows the Athenian leader, Themistocles. Despite his earlier popularity, he was ostracized from Athens in 471 BCE.

Cleisthenes also introduced a strange procedure for banishing unpopular politicians. Once a year, citizens were asked to write the name of the person they thought should be banished from the city on a fragment of broken pottery. If 6,000 votes were counted, then the individual with the greatest number of votes against him had to leave the city within ten days. He could not return to Athens for ten years, but after that period, he was allowed to resume his life as an Athenian. The system became known as ostracism from the Greek word *ostraka* (pieces of pottery).

ARISTIDES THE JUST
Even the most honourable politicians did not escape ostracism. There is a story that one citizen voted to banish Aristides because he was so tired of hearing him described as "Aristides the Just".

It is a measure of the success of Cleisthenes that his new system of government lasted for some 200 years. The Athenians seem to have had a genius for political structure, which was demonstrated by the ultimate triumph of democracy in the 5th century BCE. This would be a golden age for Athens, and an important milestone in the history of civilization.

CHAPTER SIX

The Persian wars

In the 5th century BCE, *the Greeks became involved in a series of wars with Persia, a powerful kingdom in western Asia. The Persians controlled the greatest empire in the world, stretching from Egypt and the Middle East to the borders of India.*

THE PERSIANS CAME FROM A small kingdom in the country we now know as Iran. In 547 BCE, under the leadership of Cyrus the Great, the Persian army took control of the kingdom of Lydia in Asia Minor and captured the Greek coastal cities of Ionia. Conflict arose in 499 BCE when the Ionian cities decided to revolt against their Persian masters. They drove out the tyrants who had been appointed by the Persians, and appealed to the cities of mainland Greece for help. In reply, the cities of Athens and Eretria (in Euboea) sent them men and ships. But the Greek forces were not united and were easily defeated by the might of the Persians.

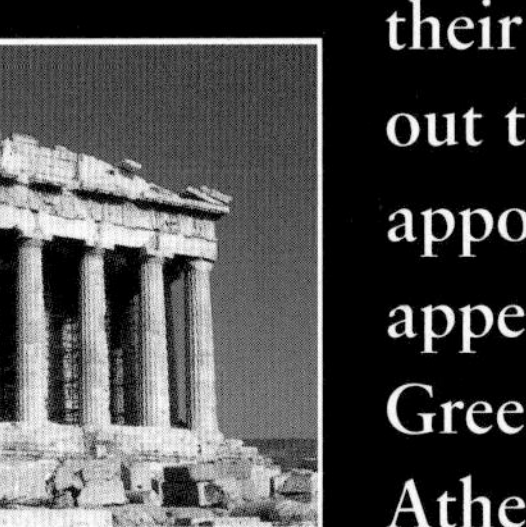

In 490 BCE, Darius I, the great king of Persia, turned his eyes towards Greece. He decided that it was time to punish those who had dared to help the rebels. It looked like an

◀ Persian soldiers from a wall sculpture in the palace at Susa, Persia

PLAN OF ATTACK
This vase, painted in the 4th century BCE, shows King Darius I of Persia making plans for campaigns of war against Greece. Darius made two unsuccessful attempts to conquer Greece.

unequal struggle – the Persians had already conquered the mighty civilizations of Egypt and Babylonia. But the Greeks were determined to fight for their independence and freedom. The Greek cities were led by the Spartans, who had previously set up a defensive alliance of southern city-states known as the Peloponnesian League. Sparta was the first city-state to realize the danger that Persia posed to the whole of Greece, and it persuaded Athens and other city-states outside the league to join forces with them against the enemy.

In 490 BCE, came the attack the Greeks had been dreading. The Persians invaded Greece with a huge force of foot soldiers and cavalry, far outnumbering any army the Greeks could assemble. The invaders travelled in ships across the Aegean Sea and landed at Marathon on the coast of Attica, just northeast of Athens. As soon as they had news of the invasion, the Athenians sent a foot messenger, Pheidippides, to run to Sparta, a distance of 233 km (145 miles), to summon help. But the Spartans were celebrating a religious festival and refused to send their army until the celebrations were over. Pheidippides then ran all the way back to Athens, and delivered the Spartans' reply. The Athenian generals decided to attack the Persians anyway, despite the fact that they were heavily outnumbered.

But if the Persians thought they would have an easy victory, they underestimated the Greek spirit. When the two armies met on the plain of Marathon, the heavily armed Athenian hoplites won a decisive victory over the Persians. In later years, it was said that the whinnying of horses and the sound of ghostly fighting men could still be heard on the plain. The Athenian army then ran back to Athens, in time to prevent the Persians from making a second landing nearer the city. This is the origin of the modern marathon, the race that is run over 40 km (26 miles), the distance from Marathon to Athens.

WEALTH OF THE EAST
This Persian bowl is made of bronze inlaid with silver. King Darius used the enormous riches of his vast empire to finance his campaigns against the Greek mainland.

As many as 6,000 Persians may have been killed in the battle of Marathon, but only 192 Athenians perished. The Persians retreated

DEADLY ENEMIES
Darius's invasion was the start of a deadly rivalry between the Greeks and the Persians. This relief is taken from the temple of Athena Nike in Athens, which was built to commemorate the victory of the Greeks over the Persians.

but Darius, angered by the unexpected defeat of his army, determined to return to Greece to crush their cities and destroy their freedom.

The effect of the Greek victory was profound and permanent. The Greeks began to see the clash between themselves and the Persians as a contest between the lovers of liberty and the supporters of tyranny. It was not quite as simple as that. The Persians had a different system of government and a different way of life, but they were not barbarians. The Persian kings ruled with great efficiency through governors called satraps. Their capital of Persepolis in Persia was famous for its splendour and its magnificence. It is said that Persian roads were so good that messengers took only seven days to travel from Susa, in the heartland of their empire, to Sardis in Asia Minor – a distance of 2,575 km (1,600 miles).

The Athenians took great pride in their victory at Marathon. Almost single-handedly their army had taken on the might of the Persian army and won. From this time forward, they became more arrogant in their attitude towards the other Greek city-states. The Athenians had a natural harbour at Piraeus, about 8 km (5 miles) from the city, and it seems likely that they had possessed a fleet from very early times. As far back as the 8th century BCE, there are pictures of warships on Athenian vases. The Athenians now made a crucially important decision to build up their fleet of triremes (long,

IMMORTAL PERSIAN
This soldier, made from glazed bricks, is one of the Immortals, the Persian king's personal bodyguards. The Immortals were so called because when one of them was killed, he was immediately replaced by a new recruit, keeping the fighting force at a constant strength of 10,000 men.

GREAT MOUND OF MARATHON
The bodies of the Athenian soldiers who died at the battle of Marathon were cremated and buried in a great mound. Each year the Athenians held a ceremony there to honour the dead.

narrow warships) so that they could rule the sea around them. They paid for these ships with the glittering wealth of the silver mines at Laurium. From now on, while the Spartan army continued to be the strongest force on land, the Athenian fleet ruled the sea.

MAJESTIC PROCESSION
The magnificent palace at Persepolis in Persia was built by Darius and his son Xerxes to reflect their power and majesty. This long procession of figures, bringing tribute from every part of the empire, lines the entrance to the great reception hall. The hall was so large that it could hold 10,000 people at a time.

GREEK TRIREME
This is *Olympias*, a replica of a Greek trireme. Triremes were very fast warships, powered in battle by 170 oarsmen. The rowers sat in three levels, one above the other, on either side of the ship.

However, within ten years of the battle of Marathon, the Greeks were forced to fight the Persians once more. Darius had died before he could launch another invasion, and the task of punishing the Greeks passed to his son, Xerxes. It took Xerxes four years to plan his attack. Instead of crossing the sea in boats, he decided to march his army overland all the way from Asia Minor through Thrace (the region bordering the northern coast of the Aegean Sea) and into northern Greece. His fleet would sail close to shore, keeping in touch with the land army. On the way, his ships would have to sail around a peninsula on the northern coast of Greece where a Persian fleet had been wrecked a few years before. So before setting out, Xerxes ordered a canal, 2.5 km (1.5 miles) long, to be dug through the peninsula. This would allow his fleet to pass through in safety.

Xerxes amassed a vast invasion force of between 200,000 and 250,000 men and 1,000 warships. It is said that his armies drank rivers dry in the course of their long journey. To cross the Hellespont (the narrow stretch of water that separates Asia Minor from Europe), he ordered two bridges to be built by lashing lines of boats together. When a storm destroyed them, he commanded that the Hellespont should be whipped 300 times, while his soldiers uttered the words "You salt and bitter stream, your master lays this punishment upon you for injuring him, who never injured you. But Xerxes the King will cross you, with or without your permission." The bridges were rebuilt, and Xerxes' huge army passed over.

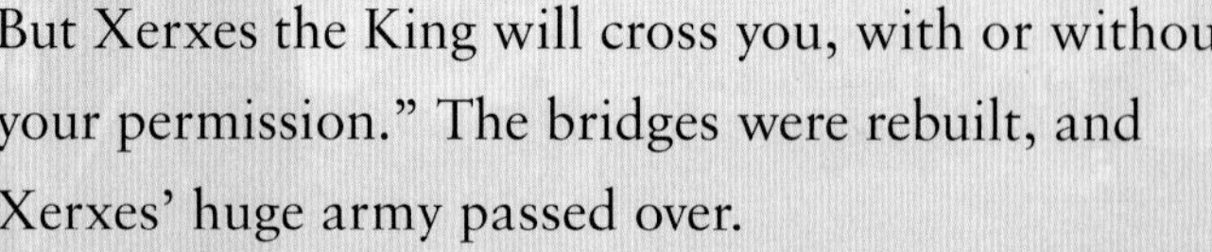

PROUD KING XERXES
This painting shows King Xerxes of Persia preparing his army to cross the Hellespont. As he travelled through Greece, Xerxes gained the support of many of the smaller Greek city-states who resented the growing power of Athens. After his humiliating defeat in battle, Xerxes left Greece and was later murdered by the captain of his bodyguard.

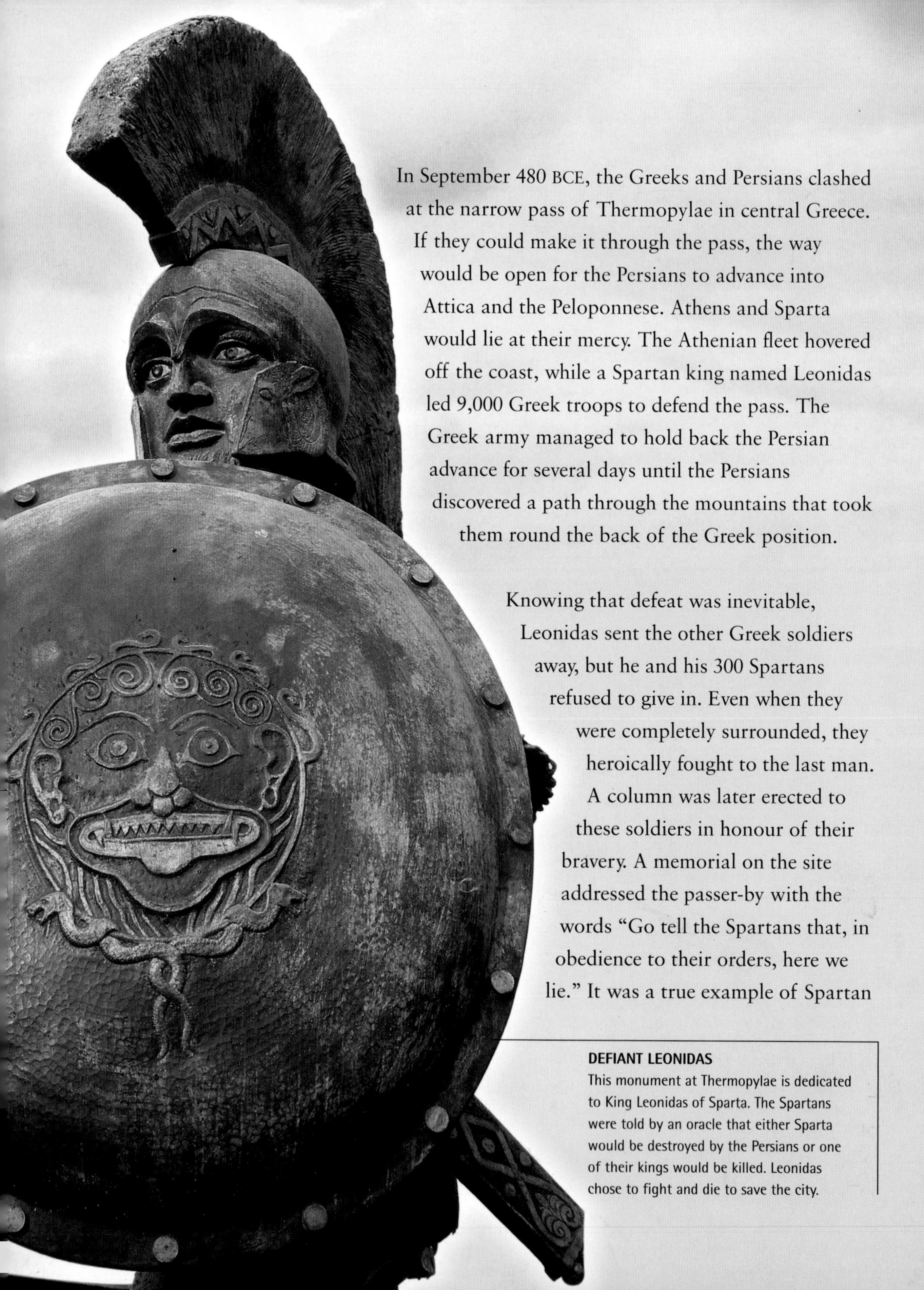

In September 480 BCE, the Greeks and Persians clashed at the narrow pass of Thermopylae in central Greece. If they could make it through the pass, the way would be open for the Persians to advance into Attica and the Peloponnese. Athens and Sparta would lie at their mercy. The Athenian fleet hovered off the coast, while a Spartan king named Leonidas led 9,000 Greek troops to defend the pass. The Greek army managed to hold back the Persian advance for several days until the Persians discovered a path through the mountains that took them round the back of the Greek position.

Knowing that defeat was inevitable, Leonidas sent the other Greek soldiers away, but he and his 300 Spartans refused to give in. Even when they were completely surrounded, they heroically fought to the last man. A column was later erected to these soldiers in honour of their bravery. A memorial on the site addressed the passer-by with the words "Go tell the Spartans that, in obedience to their orders, here we lie." It was a true example of Spartan

DEFIANT LEONIDAS
This monument at Thermopylae is dedicated to King Leonidas of Sparta. The Spartans were told by an oracle that either Sparta would be destroyed by the Persians or one of their kings would be killed. Leonidas chose to fight and die to save the city.

A bronze ram on the prow was used to sink enemy ships.

Greek warships

Athens controlled its territory by means of warships called triremes (meaning "three oars" in Latin). A trireme was a wooden ship, powered by up to 170 oarsmen, who sat on three levels inside the hull. Although triremes had sails, the Greeks always rowed into battle, because it was easier to stop, start and turn. Before battle, the sails were lowered, and the masts stowed away on deck. Built into the bow of every vessel was a long wooden ram sheathed in bronze. Each trireme aimed to crash into the back or side of an enemy ship to sink it. If that failed, the soldiers would fire arrows at the enemy from the deck. If enemy soldiers fell into the water, they either drowned or were speared like fish from above.

discipline, even in the face of certain death. Xerxes had seen at first hand how courageously the Greeks would fight for their land and for their freedom.

Having defeated the Spartans, the mighty Persian army moved southwards. Many city-states decided to make peace with the invading army, but Athens determined to fight on, relying on the strength of its fleet. Its leaders now decided to evacuate the city entirely, and to fight at sea. The citizens, with their families and slaves, were put on board ships and taken to adjacent islands. It was a bold step, but a wise one.

When the Persian army reached Athens, it found the city deserted. The invaders destroyed all the public buildings on the Acropolis and burned down the temples and shrines. Meanwhile, the Athenian fleet had withdrawn to a bay off the coast of Attica, and the Persian fleet followed them to block off any retreat. A high throne was erected for Xerxes on the shore so that he could watch the naval battle that

BURNING TEMPLES

When the Persians invaded Athens in 480 BCE, they destroyed many of its temples, including the Acropolis – an act of blasphemy that the Athenians never forgot. In 450 BCE, Pericles, an Athenian general, built a new temple called the Parthenon on the ashes of the old site.

followed. He was dismayed by what he witnessed. In a narrow channel of water by the island of Salamis, the unwieldy Persian fleet was cut off and outmanoeuvred by the Athenian ships. Trapped, then rammed by the Athenian triremes, the Persian ships were unable to turn round and were completely destroyed. Humiliated, Xerxes left the scene of the battle. It had been a tremendous victory for the Athenians, and the Battle of Salamis became famous in song, legend and drama.

SPARTAN FIGHTER
This vase painting shows a Spartan hoplite locked in combat with a Persian foot soldier. All the other Greeks were in awe of the Spartans' fighting spirit. The unity of the city-states did not last, however. Once the Persian threat was removed, the Athenians and Spartans went back to fighting each other.

Xerxes did not want to be stranded in Greece without good lines of supply, so he retraced his steps through northern Greece and Thrace, across the Hellespont and through Asia Minor back to Persia, leaving a large army of some 120,000 men in northern Greece. Knowing how readily the Greeks argued among themselves, the Persians tried to put a wedge between the Athenians and the Spartans. They sent an ambassador to Athens with an offer to rebuild the city

HONOURING THE DEAD
Greek soldiers who died defending their country were given public funerals. This vase painting shows a fallen Greek soldier seated in his tomb with his weapons and his armour. Nakedness was a symbol of heroic bravery in Greek art. In reality, soldiers wore tunics under their armour.

they had left in ruins, and to help it become the most powerful state in Greece. The Athenians sent back the defiant message that "as long as the sun moves in its present course, we will never come to terms with Xerxes."

In the summer of 479 BCE, the Greek army, led by the Spartan general Pausanias, met the Persians once more at a place called Plataea. There was a pitched battle during which the Spartan hoplites charged at the Persian soldiers in tight formation, and the Persian general was killed. Meanwhile, Greek forces destroyed the Persian fleet while it was moored at Cape Mycale of the coast of Asia Minor. It was the end of the Persian campaign.

Although the Athenians played little part in this last victory, they still portrayed it as a triumph over the barbarians by all the Greeks. They claimed that Xerxes had failed in his campaign because of his blasphemy in burning the temples of the gods on the Athenian Acropolis. In Greece, history was as much a matter of legend and story as of truth. There is no doubt, however, that both the battles of Salamis and Plataea represented great triumphs for the Greeks. The Persians would never again attempt to invade Europe.

Herodotus, father of history

The first person to write what we now call history was a man named Herodotus (c.484–c.425 BCE). He is most famous for his detailed account of the Persian Wars. Born at Halicarnassus in Ionia, he travelled widely around the Mediterranean, collecting information for his book, which brought together a wealth of geographical and anecdotal detail about the various peoples involved in the Persian Wars. Known as the "father of history", he was the first person to establish historical facts and write about them as a sequence of linked events.

CHAPTER SEVEN

The Golden Age

When the defeated Persians withdrew from Athens in 479 BCE, they left the city in ruins. But over the next 50 years, Athens was transformed into a city of glittering marble. The jewel in the city's crown was a new temple on the Acropolis – the Parthenon.

THE FINAL DEFEAT OF THE Persians greatly increased the confidence of the Athenians, who now controlled the largest and most successful navy in the world. Still fearful of future Persian attacks, the Athenians set up an alliance with other city-states on the island of Delos in the Aegean Sea. This alliance was known as the Delian League. The alliance was never really an association of equals, and it was soon completely dominated by the Athenians. They made the other members of the league put large sums of money into a treasury that was kept at the sacred sanctuary of Apollo on Delos. They also refused to allow any members to leave the league. In 454 BCE, the Athenians moved the league's treasury from Delos to the Acropolis in Athens, claiming that it would be safer there. The Delian League had turned into an Athenian empire, and Athens

◀ A bronze copy of an actor's mask

had entered a golden age of prosperity and freedom. The Athenians owed much of their success to a statesman and general named Pericles. He was elected *strategos* (military commander) every year from 443 to 429 BCE, and he was in all respects the leader of the city. A powerful orator (public speaker), Pericles was popular with the Athenian citizens, and Athens prospered under his rule.

THE PNYX
The remains of the large stone and earth platform, where the Assembly of 6,000 citizens met, are still visible on top of the Pnyx, a small hill in Athens.

Matters of policy in Athens were decided by the Assembly, which consisted of all male citizens over the age of 18. Meetings took place every ten days on a hill called the Pnyx, just west of the Acropolis. A minimum of 6,000 citizens had to be present, and all citizens, rich or poor, had the right to speak out in public. Any citizen who wished to speak was escorted to the speaker's platform. When he spoke, he kept his arms and hands within his cloak as a sign of politeness. Votes were taken on a show of hands. To make sure that enough citizens attended the Assembly, a long rope covered in red powder was used to round people up in the market place and drive them towards the Pnyx. Any citizen found

ROARING LIONS
This procession of marble lions once guarded the sanctuary of Apollo on Delos, sacred to all the Greeks. Originally there were 16 lions, but only five remain standing today. The marble used to carve the lions came from the nearby island of Naxos.

outside the Assembly with red powder on his clothes could be punished for evading his duty.

One of the duties of an Athenian citizen was to sit on a jury and hear legal cases, as there were no professional lawyers or judges in Athens. These juries were made up of hundreds, or even thousands, of people, and the jurors were paid a small sum of money each day as an encouragement to attend. Citizens were also encouraged to sit on the various boards that managed the affairs of the city. The Athenians believed that elections favoured the rich or the powerful, so the people serving on these boards were chosen by lot each year. No citizen was permitted to serve in the same post more than twice.

Only citizens were allowed a say in how the state was run. Women, slaves and metics (resident foreigners who lived and worked in Athens without being granted

MYRTLE WREATH
The Greeks used myrtle to make wreaths as its leaves grew in a symmetrical pattern. Any citizen who wished to speak at the Assembly had a myrtle wreath placed on his head as a sign of status. Gold wreaths, such as this one, were made to decorate statues of gods or were placed on the heads of corpses in tombs.

NON-CITIZENS
In Athens, metics might own businesses or work as bakers, carpenters or gardeners. These women baking bread were probably slaves, who, like metics, were denied citizen status.

citizen status) were excluded from public affairs. Many metics were highly regarded, and some grew extremely rich, but they were not part of the democracy of Athens.

In Pericles' time, there were perhaps as many as 45,000 adult male citizens, 50,000 metics and approximately 100,000 slaves in Athens. Women and children counted for another 100,000. Athens was not a full democracy, but it is the closest any state has come to that goal in human history. It set an example to the rest of Greece, where democracies began to take the place of oligarchies and tyrannies in many city-states.

The Athenians spent much of their time honouring and celebrating the gods who protected their city. The festival of the goddess Athena was celebrated with athletic games and with poetry and musical competitions. Another festival, held over a period of five days in the spring, honoured

EPIDAUROS
The theatre at Epidauros was so well designed that even those in the top row could get a clear view of the performance and hear every word spoken. The flat circular area (*orchestra)* in the foreground was where the actors performed.

Dionysus, the god of wine, and was called the Great Dionysia. During the celebrations, it became the custom for actors to perform four dramas, or plays, each day. These early plays may have developed from the ritual songs and dances that celebrated the life and death of Dionysus.

By Athens' Golden Age, the plays were performed during the day in an outdoor theatre, over a period of three days. The actors (who were all male) wore decorated costumes and masks to represent different characters, but there was very little scenery. The audience's attention was focused entirely upon the words and the characters.

One form of drama, known as tragedy, alternated long speeches (or dialogues) delivered by actors with the singing and dancing of the chorus. The chorus was a group of men who sang songs, danced and spoke as a group. They questioned the actors, commented on the action and helped to explain the play to the audience. The tragedies took their stories

PRIZE GOAT
The word tragedy literally meant "goatsong" in Greek. According to legend, the first play performed at the festival of Dionysus was written by a poet called Thespis, who received a goat as a prize.

GREAT DIONYSIA
This vase painting shows the god Dionysus donating a gift of wine. During the festival of Dionysia, processions and sacrifices were followed by drama competitions.

SOPHOCLES
Sophocles was 28 when he first won the prize at the Great Dionysia, and he was still writing plays in his 80s. Only seven of his 100 or so plays survive.

and characters from the myths and legends of Greek history, which were well known to Athenians. They dealt with themes such as justice and honour, virtue and excellence, and showed the terrible punishments that men and women bring upon themselves through pride. In the tragedies, human beings are caught in situations that will inevitably bring them to failure or ruin. For example, in *Oedipus the King*, a play written by the dramatist Sophocles, Oedipus tries everything he can think of to avoid a prophecy that claimed he would murder his father and marry his mother. But he cannot escape his destiny – that is his tragedy.

Like other ancient peoples, the Greeks were filled with anxiety and terror. They had no Bible or holy book, so drama was one of the most important ways of celebrating the sacred mysteries of human existence. The greatest Athenian dramatists were men of experience. One of them, Aeschylus, had fought at the battles of Marathon and Salamis, and Sophocles had twice been elected as a military commander. It is because they understood so well the truth of what it is to be human that the plays of these men still speak to us today.

Tragedies were not the only plays performed at the Great Dionysia festival. There were also comedies, which poked fun at the daily concerns of the Athenians. No one escaped the mocking wit of the comedies, not even the most important men of the city. In Athenian society, there was genuine freedom of speech.

The Athenians probably knew that they were living through an extraordinary period – they certainly felt themselves to be chosen by the gods. Plato, an Athenian philosopher who lived the following century, said that "the city is full of liberty and free speech, and everyone in it is allowed to do as he pleases." The Athenians lived as free citizens, and their thriving city attracted painters and poets, historians and dramatists, philosophers and orators from all over Greece.

To celebrate the growing importance of Athens, Pericles began a programme of public building that changed the face of the city. He persuaded his fellow citizens to use the funds from Athens' control of the Delian League (as well as wealth from Athens' silver mines at Laurium) to rebuild the temples destroyed 30 years earlier by the Persians. He also commissioned a new temple on the Acropolis that would rival anything ever created

COMEDY MASKS
Comic slaves and servants were favourite characters in Greek comedy. These small clay models with their grotesque masks and padded costumes represent popular comic characters.

SATYR PLAYS
This vase painting shows actors dressed up as satyrs, mythical creatures that were half-man and half-goat. Traditionally, satyrs were slaves to the god Dionysus.

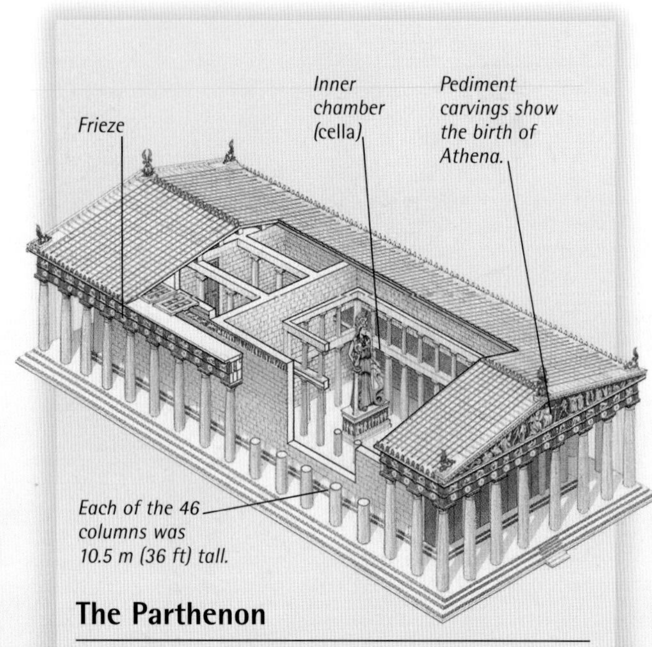

The Parthenon

The new temple on the Acropolis, the Parthenon, was built by an architect named Ictinus and was dedicated to Athena, the patron goddess of Athens. The entire building was carved from sparkling white marble and was decorated with magnificent carved stone figures, painted in bright colours. Its tall columns supported a horizontal band, or frieze, which went round all four sides of the temple. The marble frieze was decorated with scenes of mythical battles.

The goddess Athena
Inside the Parthenon stood a huge gold and ivory statue of the goddess Athena, made by the sculptor Phidias. In this replica, based on a smaller copy of the original statue, she wears her *Aegis* – a mysterious cloak fringed with snakes, and a high-crested helmet. On her right hand is a winged figure of Nike, the goddess of victory.

before. This wonderful new building was called the Parthenon, dedicated to Athena Parthenos (Athena the Virgin). Some 20,000 tonnes of marble went into its building, and it was nearly 40 m (100 ft) wide and 70 m (228 ft) long. This great temple was designed to house a colossal statue of the goddess Athena, about 12 m (39 ft) high, covered in gold and ivory. The sculptured panels and carved stone figures that decorated the building added to the overwhelming sense of beauty and majesty that the temple aroused in all who saw it.

Of course, Athenian society, like that of all the Greek city-states, was based upon the labour and produce of farmers living in village settlements. This had remained unchanged for many hundreds of years, and at least 80 per cent of the population continued to work on the land. Life on a farm was difficult, as the soil in much of Greece was of poor quality. Greek farmers ploughed in spring and

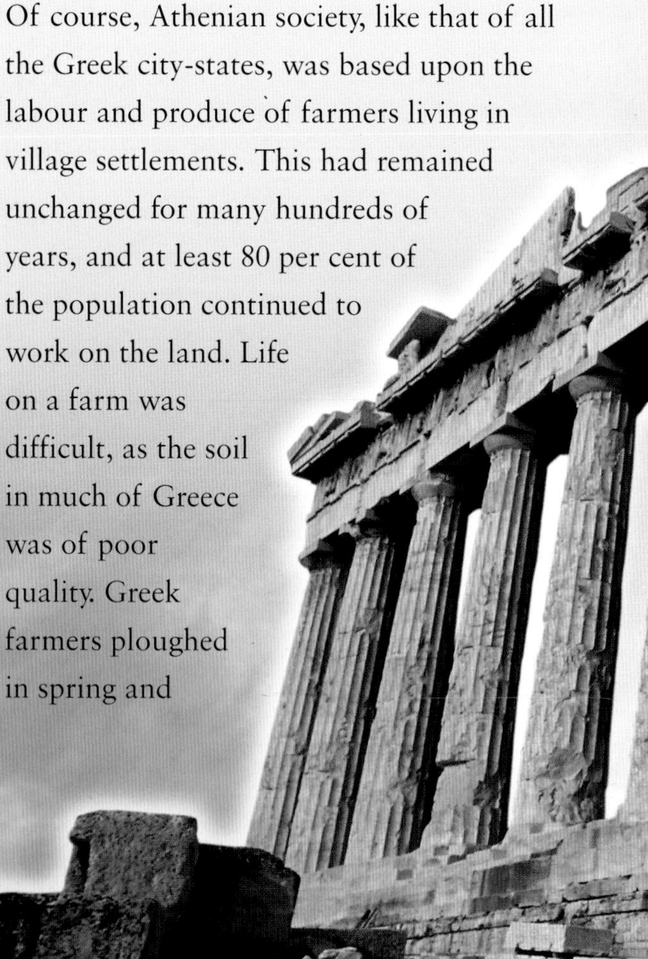

then again in autumn. Many farmers chose to live in the cities and travelled out each day to their fields and their hillsides.

CLEANING SILVER
These holes in the ground were for washing the silver ore mined at Laurium. Conditions were difficult for the slaves who had to work in narrow shafts deep below the ground. Digging out the ore and hauling it to the surface was backbreaking work, and many slaves died from exhaustion.

Although many Greek cities were ruled by democracies, that did not mean their societies were based upon equality. There was always a division between the rich and the poor in Athens, even if they shared the same privileges as citizens. It was generally understood, however, that rich citizens should give some of their wealth to the city – they might build and equip a new warship, for example, or pay for the chorus in one of the festival dramas. These donations to the city were known as "liturgies".

The daily lives of Greek men and women were very different in Greece. With the exception of the women of Sparta, Greek women led very sheltered lives. In rich Athenian families,

ATHENIAN GLORY
Constructed between 447 and 432 BCE, the Parthenon was built as a thank-you offering to the goddess Athena, who was thought to have brought the Athenians victory in the Persian Wars. Marble for the temple was cut from quarries on Mount Pentelicon and transported to Athens by wagons drawn by oxen.

FETCHING WATER
Every day, female slaves and the poorer women of Greece went to the public fountains to fill their water pots.

the women lived apart from the men in their own rooms on the upper floors, and were not allowed to mix with men at dinners or parties. Nor were they allowed to inherit money or own property. If the father of an unmarried woman died, and she was the sole heiress, then the father's closest male relative was obliged to marry her. A girl would marry very young, at the age of 13 or 14, and her husband was chosen by her father. Most of the time, wealthy Greek women were confined to the house and forbidden to go out into the streets, although they were allowed to invite female friends round and appear in public during religious festivals. All the shopping was done by men, or by slaves. But, while the women from the richer families were kept secluded, poorer women could not afford to stay indoors. They were forced to go out to work, either picking fruit or buying and selling goods in the streets or in the markets.

At home, men ruled the household in every sense. The future of a baby rested entirely in the hands of its father, and there were some parts of Greece where it was even permissible for a father to sell his children. In Athens, the law allowed a father to get rid of his unwanted newborn infant by placing it in a vase or jar and leaving it outside to die. However, adults were required to look after their elderly parents, and could

WORKING THE LAND
This carving shows a Greek farmer with his two oxen. The soil of Greece was often hard and stony, and ploughs such as this one were made of wood and sometimes tipped with iron.

GREEK DRESS
Clothes in Greece were made largely of wool provided by local sheep. Men and women of all ages and classes wore a garment called a *chiton*, made from a single rectangle of cloth.

be punished by law if they failed to do so.

Most boys worked on their father's farm or learned their father's trade as soon as they were old enough. Girls stayed at home and learned how to cook and take care of the house. Only boys from rich families went to school, from the age of seven to 18. Their teachers were often slaves, and their lessons included literature, arithmetic and physical training. They were also taught to memorize poetry and to play musical instruments such as the lyre and the pipes. At the age of 18, they had to be ready to fight in the army and, after that, in Athens and other democracies, they became full citizens with voting rights in the assemblies. In Greece, young men were taught how to be warriors as well as citizens.

The Greeks believed that it was important to keep the body as fit as possible, and both boys and adult men would visit the gymnasium to exercise and compete in a variety of different sports. Favourite sports included the

WOMEN'S WORLD
Although wealthy women were expected to stay at home, many had slaves to help them with the housework.

EDUCATION
This carving shows a school boy reading aloud from a papyrus roll. Rich boys might be taught the art of public speaking by teachers called sophists, who travelled from city to city.

LEARNING THE LYRE
Music was an essential part of a boy's education, and special teachers were hired to teach the lyre, a stringed instrument that had a tortoiseshell for a sound-box.

long jump and discus-throwing. Greek males also learned how to wrestle and to box. There were swimming pools, too, but swimming seems to have been considered a very ordinary accomplishment. But the life of a wealthy young Athenian was not all study and physical training. Children were allowed time for play, and archaeologists have found many toys, including rattles, dolls, horses on wheels, and small statuettes of animals. Children also kept pet animals, including ducks and grasshoppers.

In contrast to their fine public buildings, the private dwellings of the citizens of Athens were dull and shabby. They tended to be small, too, and the walls were very flimsy. Burglars were known as "wall-piercers" because that was the easiest way to force an entry into a house. The garden or courtyard was in the middle of the house with all the rooms arranged around it. Very few houses had their own water supply, and most people had to visit a spring or a public well.

The Greek diet was basically a simple but healthy one of cereals, vegetables, and fruit. Grapes were grown for wine, and were

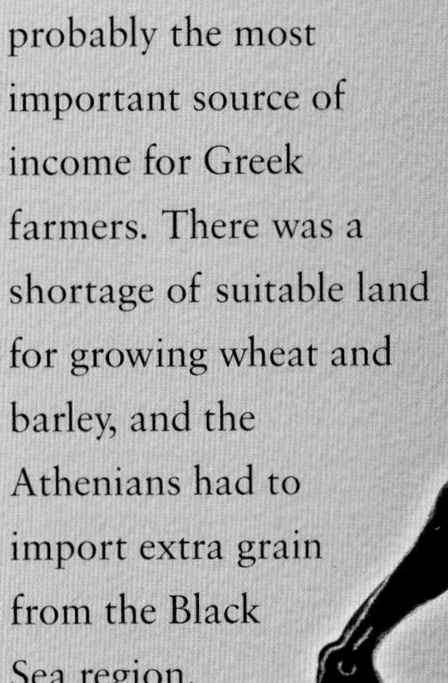

probably the most important source of income for Greek farmers. There was a shortage of suitable land for growing wheat and barley, and the Athenians had to import extra grain from the Black Sea region. Farmers reared sheep, goats, cows and pigs, but meat was reserved mostly for special occasions. The Greeks did not eat butter or drink milk – they preferred water and wine, often mixed together. Although olives were used as food, their oil was an even more vital part of Greek life, and was used for cooking and for burning as fuel in lamps. It was even used to wash the body, instead of soap. At the end of a meal, the Greeks ate sweet fruits like figs or pomegranates, or cakes sweetened with honey from the mountains of Hymettus, near Athens.

FIGHTING FOR SPORT
Wrestling matches lasted until one of the contestants surrendered out of sheer exhaustion. Wrestling was banned in Sparta, because no Spartan man was ever allowed to admit defeat.

Life expectancy was low – about 30 years – and there is evidence of malnutrition and epidemic disease. And although the life on the land must have been hard and wearisome, even the poorest citizens took part in leisure pursuits such as dice or cock-fighting. Many Greeks enjoyed the game of knucklebones in which

HOUSE IN THE COUNTRY
The walls of this simple farmhouse are made of sun-dried bricks covered in plaster. The windows are small with wooden shutters, and the roof is covered with clay tiles.

HEALTHY EATING
The Greek diet was simple and healthy and included lots of pulses such as chickpeas and lentils. Figs and nuts were eaten at the end of a meal.

small animal bones were thrown like dice. The rich enjoyed hunting and sports, as well as lavish entertaining. One favourite Athenian entertainment was called a symposium, or drinking party. The guests reclined on couches while slaves poured them a mixture of wine and water. All respectable women were excluded from a symposium, but slave girls, called hetairai, would entertain men with dancing and flute-playing.

DAILY BREAD
Bread was eaten every day, made at home by women or kitchen slaves. It could also be bought from bakers in the market place.

Slaves made up the largest part of the population of Athens. They were either prisoners of war or barbarians (non-Greeks) who had been captured and sold in the market place. Many of them were tattooed or branded, so that their owner could be easily recognized. The treatment of slaves was often cruel – for example, the slaves who worked for pastry-cooks were muzzled so they could not eat anything. In the silver mines of Laurium, from which Athens received much of its income, there may have been up to 30,000 slaves, forced to endure the most terrible conditions. Some of the tunnels at Laurium were so small that only children could work within them.

DRINKING PARTY
This vase painting shows a banqueting scene, in which a slave girl entertains the reclining diners by playing music on the double pipes.

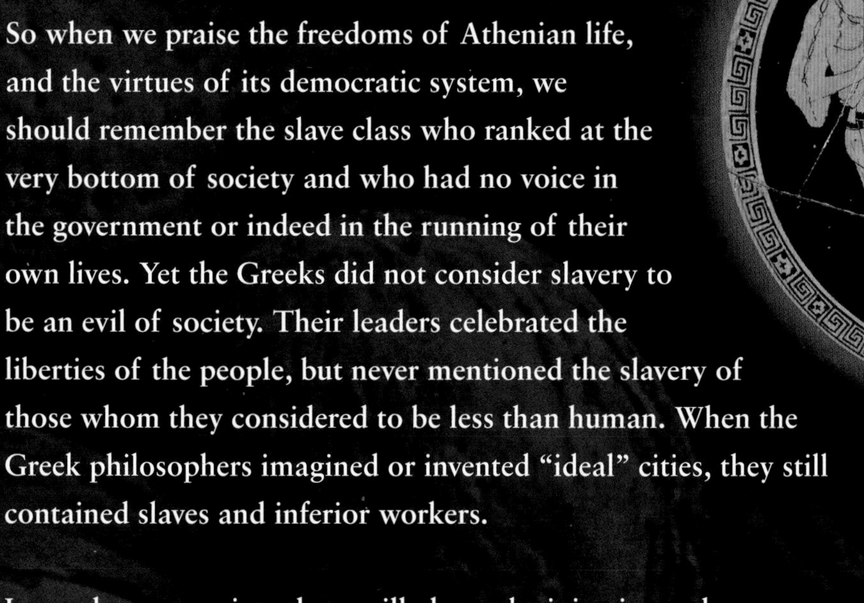

So when we praise the freedoms of Athenian life, and the virtues of its democratic system, we should remember the slave class who ranked at the very bottom of society and who had no voice in the government or indeed in the running of their own lives. Yet the Greeks did not consider slavery to be an evil of society. Their leaders celebrated the liberties of the people, but never mentioned the slavery of those whom they considered to be less than human. When the Greek philosophers imagined or invented "ideal" cities, they still contained slaves and inferior workers.

In any human society there will always be injustice and even inhumanity, at the same time as there is generosity or goodness. And for all its shortcomings, the democratic society and civilized life enjoyed in Athens during its Golden Age has remained an inspiration and an ideal to the world ever since.

MASTER AND SLAVE
In this painting, a slave serves wine to her master. Most of the housework done in wealthy Greek homes was carried out by slaves, who often became trusted members of the family.

CHAPTER EIGHT

Cities at war

Under the leadership of Pericles, the city of Athens had become wealthy and powerful. Other city-states began to feel threatened, and war finally broke out in 431 BCE. The Peloponnesian War, which lasted for 27 years, ended in the defeat of Athens.

THE GREATEST WARRIOR STATE of all was Sparta. It had watched with growing suspicion and alarm as Athens used its fleet to establish an empire at sea. After a series of battles and skirmishes between Athens and the allies of Sparta, both sides signed a truce in 445 BCE. But cities with such different characters and ambitions could not remain at peace for long. Sparta was governed by an oligarchy (the rule of a few), whereas Athens had a full-fledged democracy. Athens, through its harbour at Piraeus, was open to all the traffic and trade of the Mediterranean world, whereas Sparta was secluded in a remote valley. Athens led the world in drama, sculpture and architecture, whereas Spartans cared little for such things. The two cities were natural enemies for all these reasons, but it was the growth of Athenian power that led Sparta to break the truce.

◀ Aphrodite, goddess of love, pouring wine for Ares, god of war

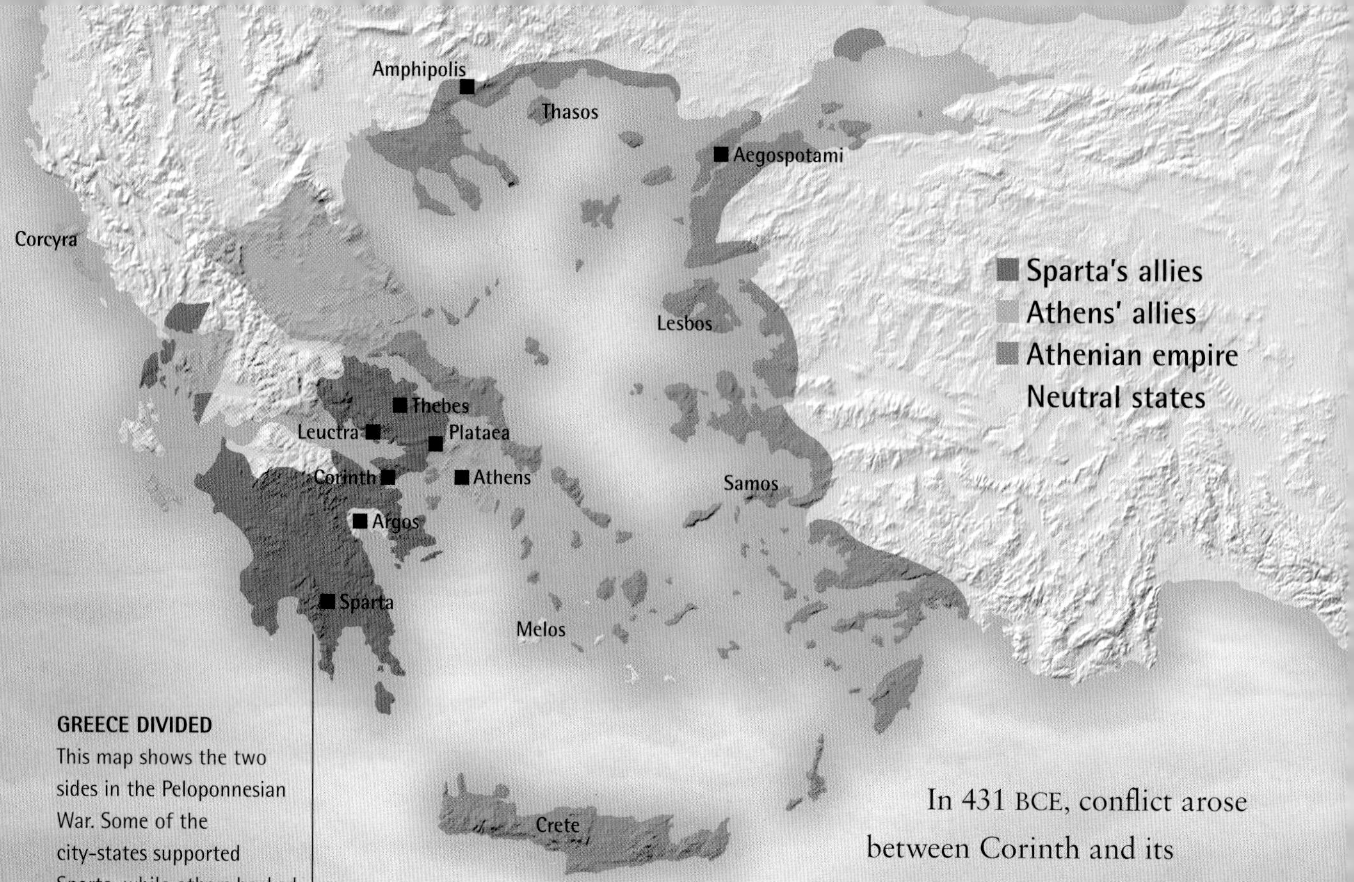

Amphipolis
Thasos
Aegospotami
Corcyra
Lesbos
Thebes
Leuctra
Plataea
Corinth
Athens
Samos
Argos
Sparta
Melos
Crete

Sparta's allies
Athens' allies
Athenian empire
Neutral states

GREECE DIVIDED
This map shows the two sides in the Peloponnesian War. Some of the city-states supported Sparta, while others backed Athens and its empire.

In 431 BCE, conflict arose between Corinth and its colony of Corcyra (Corfu). Sparta and Athens supported opposing sides. That same year, Sparta declared war on Athens and invaded Attica, so beginning the Peloponnesian War that lasted 27 years.

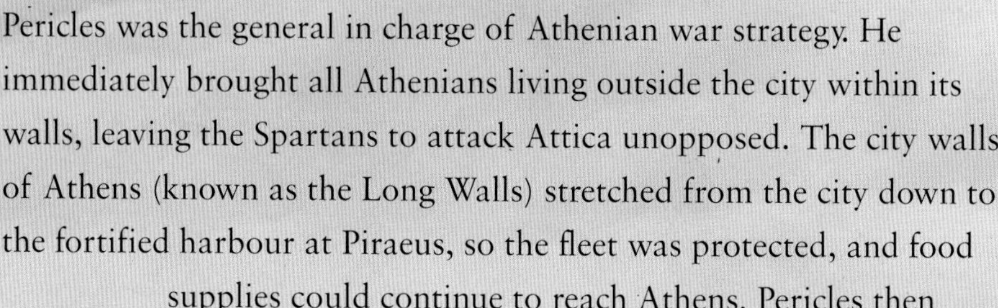

Pericles was the general in charge of Athenian war strategy. He immediately brought all Athenians living outside the city within its walls, leaving the Spartans to attack Attica unopposed. The city walls of Athens (known as the Long Walls) stretched from the city down to the fortified harbour at Piraeus, so the fleet was protected, and food supplies could continue to reach Athens. Pericles then used the large Athenian fleet to launch attacks around the Peloponnesian coast. He hoped to be able to wear the enemy down until Sparta's allies became disheartened and went over to the Athenian side. He also hoped to persuade the helots to revolt against Sparta.

HARBOUR OF PIRAEUS
This is a modern-day view of the harbour of Piraeus. In the 5th century BCE, two long stone walls connected the fortified port and naval base at Piraeus to Athens 11 km (7 miles) away. As long as its fleet controlled the sea, Athens could not be starved into surrender.

After the first year of warfare, there was a public funeral for the dead, during which Pericles made a stirring speech in praise of Athens and its people. It has become one of the most famous speeches ever made: "We are lovers of the beautiful," he proclaimed, "yet simple in our tastes, and we cultivate the mind without loss of manliness. It is no disgrace with us to confess poverty; the true disgrace is to do nothing to avoid it."

PERICLES, ATHENIAN GENERAL
Pericles dominated Athens for 20 years, when the city's wealth and power was at its height. This bust, a Roman copy, was made not long before his death in 429 BCE.

During the course of the war, Athens became a refugee camp for many thousands of people. Because there was not enough room to house all the families that moved from the country into the city, many had to live in the street or in makeshift hovels. The conditions were hot, overcrowded and unhealthy. It was not long before an epidemic of plague spread through Athens, killing between a third and a quarter of the population. Pericles himself fell victim to the plague in 429 BCE, and the loss of his wise leadership may have led to some of the rash decisions that were to follow.

While the Athenians remained behind their city walls, the Spartans continued to attack the area around them. The conflict dragged on,

FUNERAL PROCESSION
On this vase, male relatives of the deceased, wearing black, carried the coffin for burial outside the city. A procession of mourners followed them. Soldiers killed in battle were given public funerals each year, and the whole city went into mourning.

KILLED IN BATTLE
This sculptured relief from a tomb shows two Athenian hoplites, called Chairedemos and Lykeas, who died in battle during the Peloponnesian War.

until both sides were exhausted. In 421 BCE, Athens and Sparta signed a truce, each agreeing to give up the gains they had made.

But Athens and Sparta could never be at peace for long. In 414 BCE, the Athenians made a disastrous mistake, which proved to be a turning point in the war. It concerned Sicily, the large island by the heel of Italy. Segesta, one of the independent Greek cities in Sicily, was an ally of Athens. In 416 BCE, it appealed to the Athenians for help against its neighbour, Syracuse, the largest city in Sicily. The Athenians made a plan to conquer Syracuse, and thus gain control over Sicily and its valuable exports of grain.

So in 415 BCE, a fleet of more than 100 warships, carrying more than 5,000 soldiers, set sail for Italy with high hopes. But the three Athenian commanders argued over strategy and tactics, and the expedition was a disaster.

SICILIAN TEMPLE
The temple at Segesta was built only a few years before the Sicilian city made its appeal to Athens for military aid. It is a magnificent example of a Doric-style temple with its thick, undecorated columns.

Syracuse's fleet destroyed much of the Athenian navy, and the Athenian army was heavily defeated on land. As they retreated, thousands of Athenian soldiers were attacked and killed. Those who were captured were put to work in the stone quarries of Sicily. One of the Athenian commanders fled to Sparta, but the other two were tortured and put to death. It was the greatest humiliation that Athens had ever suffered. The city's navy was in ruins, its soldiers killed or missing, and its finances in chaos.

Most Greeks believed that the end of Athens was in sight. For a while, democracy broke down in Athens when a group of 400 oligarchs seized power in the city. However, they were unable to improve Athens' fortunes and were soon ousted by the citizens. Democracy was eventually restored, but Sparta and Athens were soon at war again.

The Spartans knew that, in order to defeat Athens, they needed to build a strong fleet of ships. So they joined forces with the Persians, who were ever willing to interfere in the quarrels of the

SYRACUSE THE GREAT
Syracuse was the second largest city in the Greek world after Athens. The face on this silver coin is of Arethusa, the patron goddess of Syracuse. Arethusa was a water nymph who was changed into a stream by the goddess Artemis to save her from the clutches of an amorous river god.

Greeks. With the gold from their former Persian enemies, the Spartans built a fleet of warships. They were now ready to attack the Athenians at sea, as well as on land. First, the Spartans seized a fort in Attica, in Athens' own territory, which gave them control of the silver mines at Laurium. Then, under the command of their admiral Lysander, they destroyed most of the Athenian navy in a surprise attack at Aegospotami in the northeast Aegean. Meanwhile, a Spartan army marched into Attica, while the Spartan navy waited at the harbour of Piraeus. Without their fleet, the Athenians could not import food into the city and faced starvation. Athens surrendered in 404 BCE, bringing an end to the long Peloponnesian War.

It was a devastating defeat. Many of Sparta's allies demanded that Athens should be totally destroyed, but the Spartans thought it would be dishonourable to extinguish a city-state that had once fought so valiantly for Greek freedom. Instead, they ordered the Athenians to pull down their walls and to surrender what remained of their navy. After its defeat, Athens was ruled by a group of pro-Spartan citizens, known as the "Thirty Tyrants". The city had never been so weak or so

ATHENIAN HOPLITE
All citizens were liable for military service, but hoplites were recruited from those who owned their own land. They were expected to provide their own armour and equipment.

PERSIAN GOLD
The winged lion was a recurrent figure in Persian art. This snarling gold lion probably came from one of the richly furnished palaces in Persia. The Persians used their vast wealth to help the Spartans in the Peloponnesian War.

WAR HISTORIAN
Thucydides, an Athenian general, wrote an 8-volume history of the Peloponnesian War after he had been exiled for losing a battle against the Spartans. It is regarded as one of the greatest histories of all time.

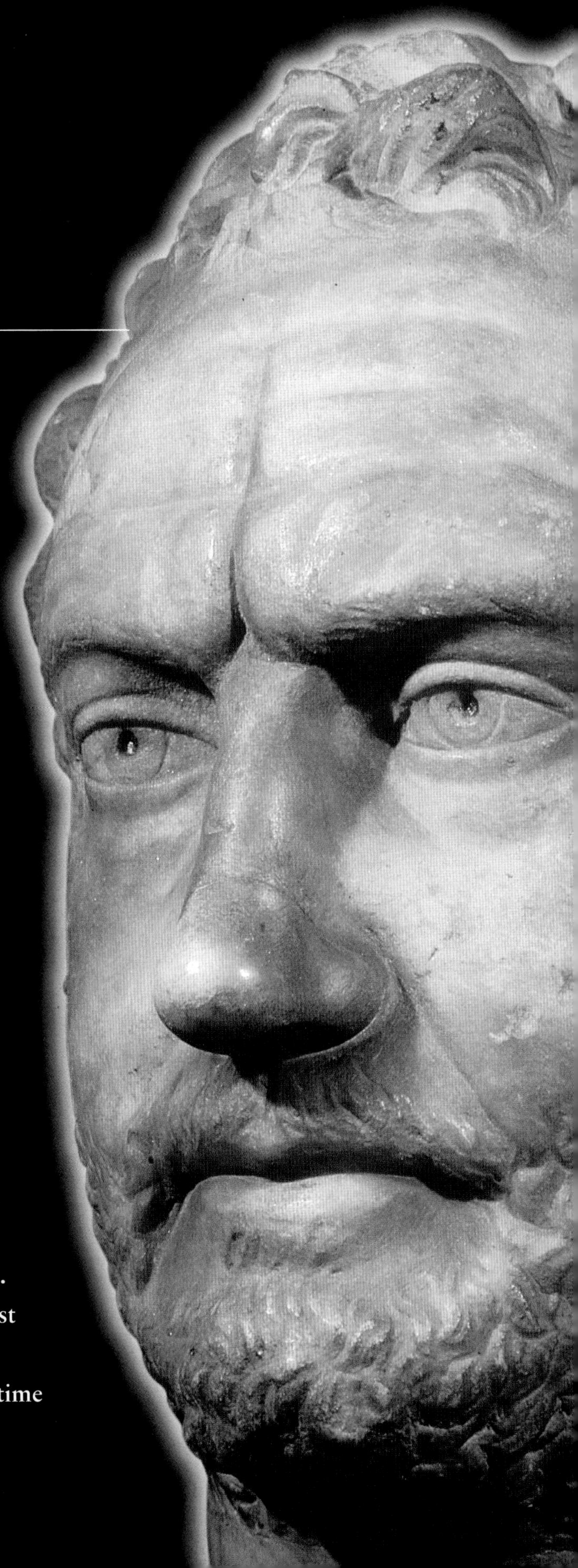

demoralized. But although Sparta had won the war, it did not win the peace. The Athenian people, resourceful as ever, threw off the rule of the tyrants after a year.

Sparta's supremacy did not last. The alliance between Sparta and Persia collapsed and, in 395 BCE, the cities of Athens and Thebes joined a new Persian alliance against Sparta. However, when the Persians saw that Athens was starting to build up its fleet again, they withdrew their support from the alliance and demanded that the Greek cities sign the King's Peace, in which the terms were dictated by the king of Persia. It was a sign of what little power the Greeks now possessed in the face of their old enemy.

Even so, the fighting did not stop. In 371 BCE, the Spartan army suffered its first major defeat in 200 years, at the hands of a Theban army at the Battle of Leuctra. This humiliating defeat marked the end of Sparta's period of greatness. The helots took the opportunity to rebel against their hated masters and set up an independent city-state under Theban protection. From this time forward, Sparta's power declined.

CHAPTER NINE

The Philosophers

Despite its setbacks and defeats, Athens continued to be the centre of culture in Greece. In the years that followed the Peloponnesian War, three of the most significant thinkers in history lived and taught in Athens. They were Socrates, Plato and Aristotle.

THE WORD PHILOSOPHY comes from the Greek word *philosophos*, which means "lover of wisdom". The first philosophers came from the region known as Ionia in eastern Greece in the 5th and 6th centuries BCE. These early scholars were the first people to ask questions about the world and how it worked, instead of simply repeating myths and stories.

One of the first Greek philosophers was Thales of Miletus who studied maths and astronomy in Egypt. He looked for answers based on reason and observation and was the first philosopher to predict an eclipse. He was supposedly so absent-minded that he fell down a well while gazing at the stars – a suitable place for him, since he believed that everything in the world was derived from water.

◀ The Academy of Plato in Athens, from a Roman mosaic

would end. Socrates, the first of the great Athenian philosophers, was interested in human behaviour and moral values. He wanted to find out what made a person good or wicked, and how people should behave in society. He valued human intelligence and open discussion and, through his teachings, he tried to show people how to live a good and virtuous life. Most importantly, he believed that he could only comment on the actions of others if he fully understood himself. He was the first philosopher to understand the importance of questioning one's own actions and beliefs.

HEAVEN AND EARTH
The philosophers looked at the stars and the planets and asked questions about the universe. They also studied the Earth, which they called *Ge*, and invented geometry and geography.

Socrates believed that we should never rely on anyone else or take anything for granted, but come to our own conclusions. He also believed that, to live a good life, we must understand the importance of virtue and follow it like a light in the night. Socrates never called himself a philosopher. He was a great teacher, but he lived and died in poverty because he refused to take any money for his lessons.

PYTHAGORAS, THE MYSTIC
Pythagoras argued that, at death, the soul of one creature passed into another body. He refused to eat meat in case a human soul was inhabiting the body of the animal he was consuming.

He wore the same cloak all the year round and walked round barefoot.

Socrates never wrote anything down. He developed his ideas in conversations with his pupils and fellow citizens, asking them such questions as "What is a good life?" and "What is justice?" He claimed that he knew nothing at all, and that his wisdom lay in realizing his own ignorance. He adopted the habit of cross-questioning his pupils and exposing the flaws in their thinking. By examining their mistakes, he hoped they might arrive together at the truth.

In the unhappy times after the downfall of the Thirty Tyrants, there were many people who thought Socrates' ideas were dangerous. In 399 BCE, he was put on trial, charged with impiety (refusing to believe in the gods) and corrupting the youth of Athens. The reality was that he had made political enemies by his habit of asking difficult questions and mocking those he debated with. Socrates could have paid a fine to avoid a trial, but he made no attempt to defend himself, claiming that he had done nothing wrong. At the end of his trial, Socrates was condemned to death.

PYTHAGORAS'S THEOREM
Pythagoras showed that if you know the lengths of two sides of a right-handed triangle, you can work out the length of a third. His proposition, shown below, is known as Pythagoras's theorem.

$$x^2 + y^2 = z^2$$

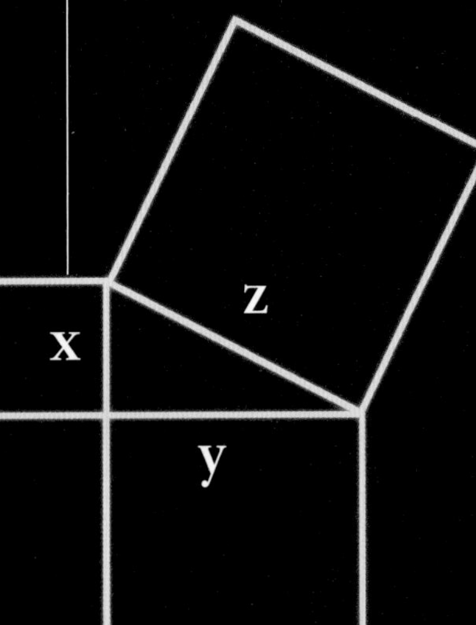

His friends begged him to flee the city, but he refused, claiming that he had lived in Athens all his life and would abide by its laws. On the day of his death, he was still calmly discussing matters of philosophy, including the immortality of the soul. It was his belief that nothing evil could happen to a good man, whether in life or in death. He was soon to find out. He was given the poison hemlock to drink, and died quickly.

DEADLY POISON
One form of execution in Greece required the victim to take a drink containing the herb hemlock. The roots and leaves of the hemlock plant contain toxins that paralyse the body's nervous system. Death follows soon after.

We owe our knowledge of Socrates' life and ideas to his pupil and fellow philosopher, Plato. After Socrates was sentenced to death, Plato left Athens. On his return, he wrote a series of books, called dialogues, in which he set out Socrates' arguments in the form of conversations with other thinkers. In 388 BCE, Plato set up his own school, the Academy, just outside Athens, where his teaching inspired many young Greeks. The Academy was famous throughout the ancient world and continued for centuries after his death.

DEATH OF SOCRATES
Plato describes how Socrates, surrounded by his friends, took the cup of poison from the executioner and waited calmly for death, a scene recreated in this 17th-century painting.

Plato wrote on many subjects, such as the nature of love and the nature of justice, but perhaps his most famous book is *The Republic,* in which he tried to imagine what a perfect society would be like.

THE THINKER
This statue shows Plato, the disciple of Socrates. Plato was an idealist – he believed that the everyday world was the shadow of a perfect, or ideal, world that exists beyond our senses.

He believed that a perfect society would be ruled by a "philosopher king" and governed by a group of wise people known as the "guardians". There would be no private property, and all children would be brought up together so that no parent knew his or her own child. Plato did not like democracy, despite the fact that he lived and worked in Athens, saying that it was the worst kind of rule. But he was writing at a time when democracy had been weakened and discredited by Athens' defeats and the political upheavals that followed.

Plato's most famous pupil was Aristotle, who was born in northern Greece and came to Athens in 367 BCE to study at the Academy. It is said that Plato used to call him "the Mind". Aristotle believed that the best way for humans to behave was the "mean" or middle way, avoiding extremes of every kind. He had a passion for nature, which he studied in a logical and methodical way. Aristotle did not believe in theories until they had been proved by observation. In other words, he was one of the first men to employ a scientific method to his studies.

Hippocrates, father of medicine

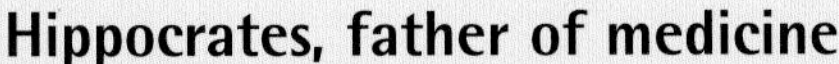

The famous Greek physician, Hippocrates (460–377 BCE), believed that illness had physical causes, and that diet and rest were important in treating disease. The "Hippocratic Oath" is still recognized as a guide to how doctors should treat their patients. Hippocrates believed that the world was made up of four elements – fire, air, earth and water – and that four fluids (humours) within the body corresponded to these four elements and to the four seasons. An "ideal" person bore all four humours in equal proportion.

MOIST
Blood
Spring
HOT
FIRE
Phlegm
Winter
WATER
AIR
Yellow bile
Summer
EARTH
COLD
Black bile
Autumn
DRY

The four humours
The philosopher Aristotle believed that most people have an excess of one or more humours, which gives each person their character. An excess of bile, for example, might make a person choleric, or bad-tempered.

Marshmallow *was used to cure stomach upsets.*

Hyssop *was used to cure pleurisy.*

Yarrow *was used by soldiers to help staunch bleeding.*

Herbal medicine
Early Greeks believed that Asclepius, the god of healing, would help them in times of illness. Hippocrates classified herbs as having hot, dry, cold and moist properties, and he was the first man to prescribe herbal medicines to prevent and cure particular diseases.

He identified more than 500 species of animal and observed their physical structure and the way they moved. He also wrote about drama and rhetoric (the power of persuasive speech). In 335 BCE, Aristotle set up a school in Athens called the Lyceum, and pupils came from all over Greece to be taught by him.

Philosophers such as Socrates, Plato and Aristotle represented a revival in Athenian learning, and re-established Athens as the cultural centre of Greece. Once more, Athens had become the city where people came to learn and to teach. Athens may have lost its empire, but it had not lost its influence.

THE SCHOOL OF ATHENS
At the centre of this fresco by the Italian painter Raphael are the philosophers Plato and Aristotle, leading lights of a group of Athenian philosophers who lived during the period of the city's greatest cultural expansion.

CHAPTER TEN

The age of Alexander

In the 4th century BCE, a new threat was developing on the northern frontier of Greece. In a mountainous country called Macedon, a ruler was emerging who would bring all of Greece under his sway. His name was Philip II.

TO THE GREEK CITY-STATES, worn out by their own wars and quarrels, Philip may not have seemed a real threat. The Macedonians were of Greek descent, but most Greeks regarded Macedon as a poor and backward country, inhabited by people who were little more than barbarians. Unlike the Greek city-states, which were mostly governed by the citizens themselves, Macedon was ruled by kings. The plains of Macedon, where the king's rule was the strongest, were occupied by people who spoke Greek. Upper Macedon was hilly country and home to warrior tribes who spoke various languages.

Philip's first achievement was to unite the people of Macedon and turn the warrior tribes into a professional army under his command. The Macedonians had always

◀ Roman mosaic showing Darius III at the Battle of Issus

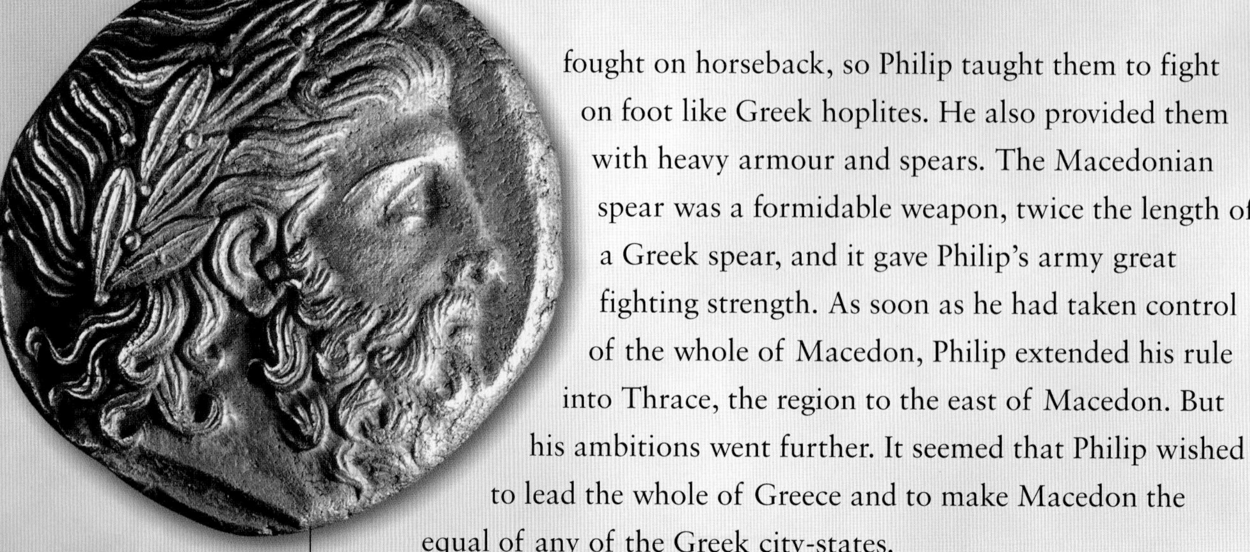

fought on horseback, so Philip taught them to fight on foot like Greek hoplites. He also provided them with heavy armour and spears. The Macedonian spear was a formidable weapon, twice the length of a Greek spear, and it gave Philip's army great fighting strength. As soon as he had taken control of the whole of Macedon, Philip extended his rule into Thrace, the region to the east of Macedon. But his ambitions went further. It seemed that Philip wished to lead the whole of Greece and to make Macedon the equal of any of the Greek city-states.

PHILIP OF MACEDON
Philip was a brilliant and ambitious ruler. When he came to the throne, his kingdom was small, weak and surrounded by enemies. By the end of his reign, he had made himself ruler of Greece.

WARRIOR RITES
The forests of Macedon were full of wild boars. A Macedonian warrior was not permitted to eat with other men until he had slaughtered one of these ferocious beasts.

Yet, first, he had to impose his rule and his will upon the rest of Greece. There were many Greeks who distrusted and feared Philip's ambition, believing that the independence of the city-states would disappear under his leadership. But there were others who welcomed his intervention in the affairs of the city-states. Philip probably bribed some leaders over to his side, but others genuinely wanted him to succeed. Some argued that it was necessary for Greece to be united under a strong ruler who could lead the country into a war against Persia. If Philip led an expedition to destroy Persia, he would be welcomed as the saviour of the Greek world.

Those states closest to Macedon tended to be more sympathetic to Philip than those further away. His reputation as a courageous and ruthless military commander went before him, and he was generally welcomed into central Greece. Some Athenian politicians were less impressed. But, as one Athenian statesman pointed out, to gain an empire in Thrace, Philip had an eye knocked out, his shoulder broken, and his legs and arms maimed. Although Philip won most of his victories by diplomacy, he would fight if he had to.

As Philip's influence spread through Greece, the Athenians and Thebans became increasingly alarmed and finally decided to oppose him in battle. In 338 BCE, the two armies met in Theban territory, at a place called Chaeronea. Philip won a crushing victory. The days of the Greek city-state seemed to be finally over. Philip summoned representatives from all the Greek cities to meet with him in Corinth and forced them to join an alliance with him, known as the League of Corinth. As the leader of the league, he would decide all policy.

Philip now announced his intention of leading a war against the Persian empire. He said that his purpose was to punish Persia for its blasphemy in destroying the temples of Greece at the time of Xerxes' invasion 150 years earlier. Before he could begin this great enterprise, however, Philip was assassinated at a wedding feast in honour of his daughter. No one knows who was responsible for his death, but it is possible that his former wife Olympias was involved in the plot.

ARISTOTLE, THE TEACHER

Philip held the culture and learning of Athens with great respect. He persuaded the great Athenian philosopher Aristotle to come to Macedon to teach his 13-year-old son Alexander, who later became Alexander the Great. Aristotle was an expert in all the sciences as well as in politics, and Alexander came to share his tutor's curiosity about the natural world.

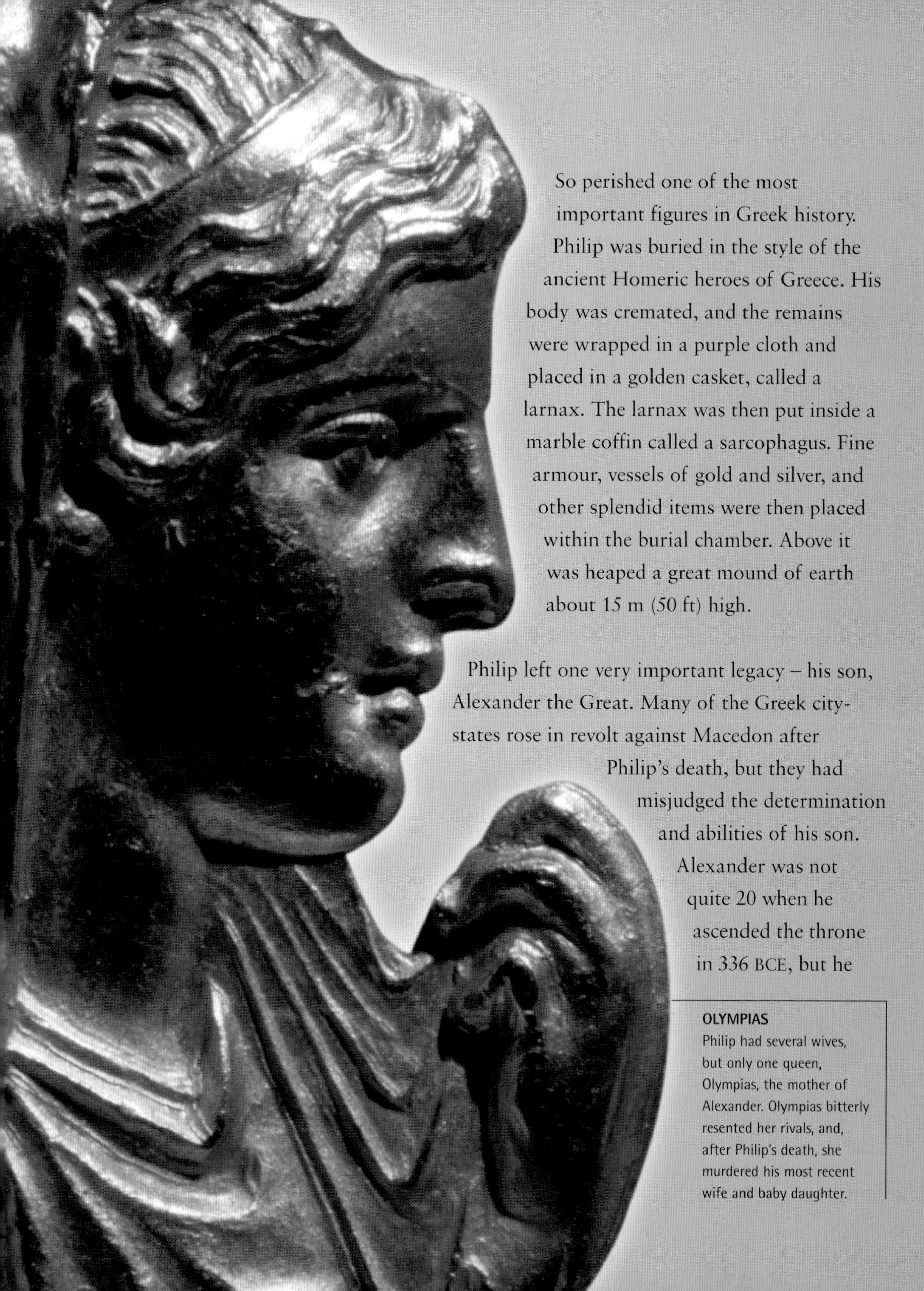

So perished one of the most important figures in Greek history. Philip was buried in the style of the ancient Homeric heroes of Greece. His body was cremated, and the remains were wrapped in a purple cloth and placed in a golden casket, called a larnax. The larnax was then put inside a marble coffin called a sarcophagus. Fine armour, vessels of gold and silver, and other splendid items were then placed within the burial chamber. Above it was heaped a great mound of earth about 15 m (50 ft) high.

Philip left one very important legacy – his son, Alexander the Great. Many of the Greek city-states rose in revolt against Macedon after Philip's death, but they had misjudged the determination and abilities of his son. Alexander was not quite 20 when he ascended the throne in 336 BCE, but he

OLYMPIAS

Philip had several wives, but only one queen, Olympias, the mother of Alexander. Olympias bitterly resented her rivals, and, after Philip's death, she murdered his most recent wife and baby daughter.

had the sense and judgment of a much older man. He also had the courage and energy of a young man.

BURIED ARMOUR
Philip was buried with a magnificent set of armour, including this fine breast plate studded with gold lion heads. His tomb also contained a golden quiver for arrows and two gilt greaves (shin guards).

Alexander marched into central Greece and quickly put down the revolt without bloodshed. He then left to fight a campaign on Macedon's northern frontier, but when Thebes rebelled again, he returned immediately and camped outside its walls. The Thebans refused to surrender, so Alexander's soldiers stormed the city. All the buildings in Thebes were razed to the ground and its inhabitants sold into slavery. The city no longer existed. It was a deliberate act of terror designed to impress his power and authority upon the rest of Greece. In this, he triumphantly succeeded, and all the city-states yielded to him.

With Greece securely conquered, Alexander now took up his father's ambition of invading the Persian empire. Yet his plans went further than Philip had have ever dreamed of. He sold off most of his land and property before setting out on his long campaign. When asked what he had left, Alexander replied, "My hopes."

In 334 BCE, Alexander led his vast army of 37,000 men across the Hellespont channel into Asia. Near the site of the fabled

TOMB OF A WARRIOR KING
In 1977, archaeologists discovered a tomb at Vergina in Macedonia, which they believed belonged to Philip II. Unlike most ancient tombs, Philip's grave had never been robbed. The armour and tableware was found exactly where it had been placed at Philip's funeral in 336 BCE.

Fall of Thebes

The city of Thebes lay northwest of Athens in the central part of Boeotia in eastern Greece. Originally a Mycenaean city, the "seven-gated city of Thebes" was the seat of one of the oldest and greatest powers of Greece. The city was originally named Cadmeia, after Cadmus, its mythical founder and first king. During the Peloponnesian Wars, it was allied with Sparta against Athens and, for a short time after 371 BCE, when Thebes defeated Sparta at Leuctra, it was the most powerful city-state in Greece. A revolt at Thebes caused Alexander the Great to attack and destroy the city in 336 BCE. It was rebuilt in 315 BCE, but it never regained its former greatness.

Alexander's destruction of Thebes

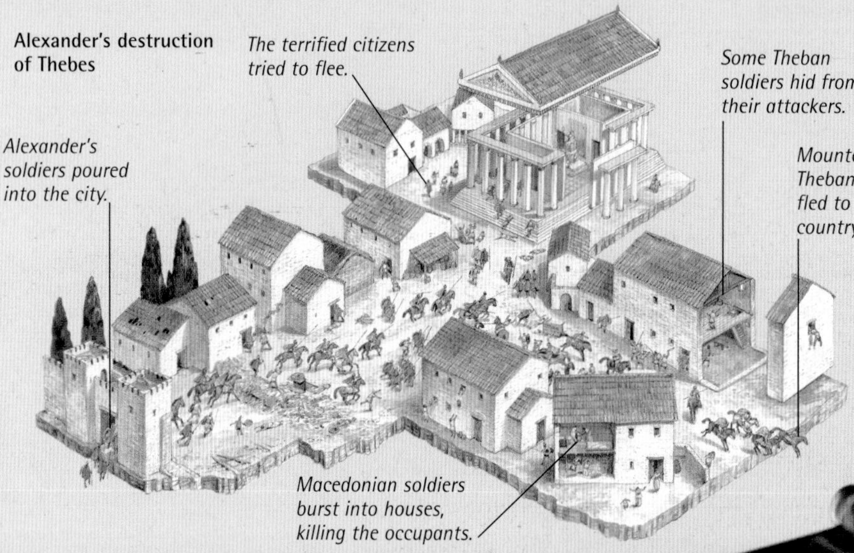

The terrified citizens tried to flee.

Some Theban soldiers hid from their attackers.

Alexander's soldiers poured into the city.

Mounted Theban troops fled to the countryside.

Macedonian soldiers burst into houses, killing the occupants.

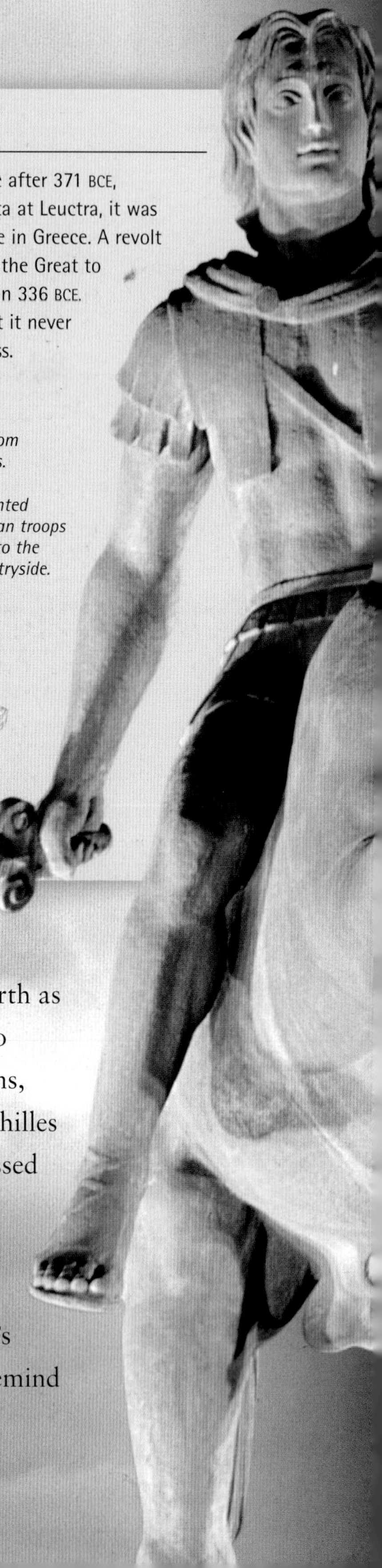

city of Troy, he hurled his spear into the earth as a sign of conquest and dedicated himself to Athena, the goddess of war. By these actions, Alexander was associating himself with Achilles and the other Greek warriors who had crossed into Asia and defeated the Trojans.

Alexander modelled himself on the ancient heroes of Greek legend. It is said that he always slept with a copy of Homer's epic poem the *Iliad* beneath his pillow to remind him of their great acts of bravery.

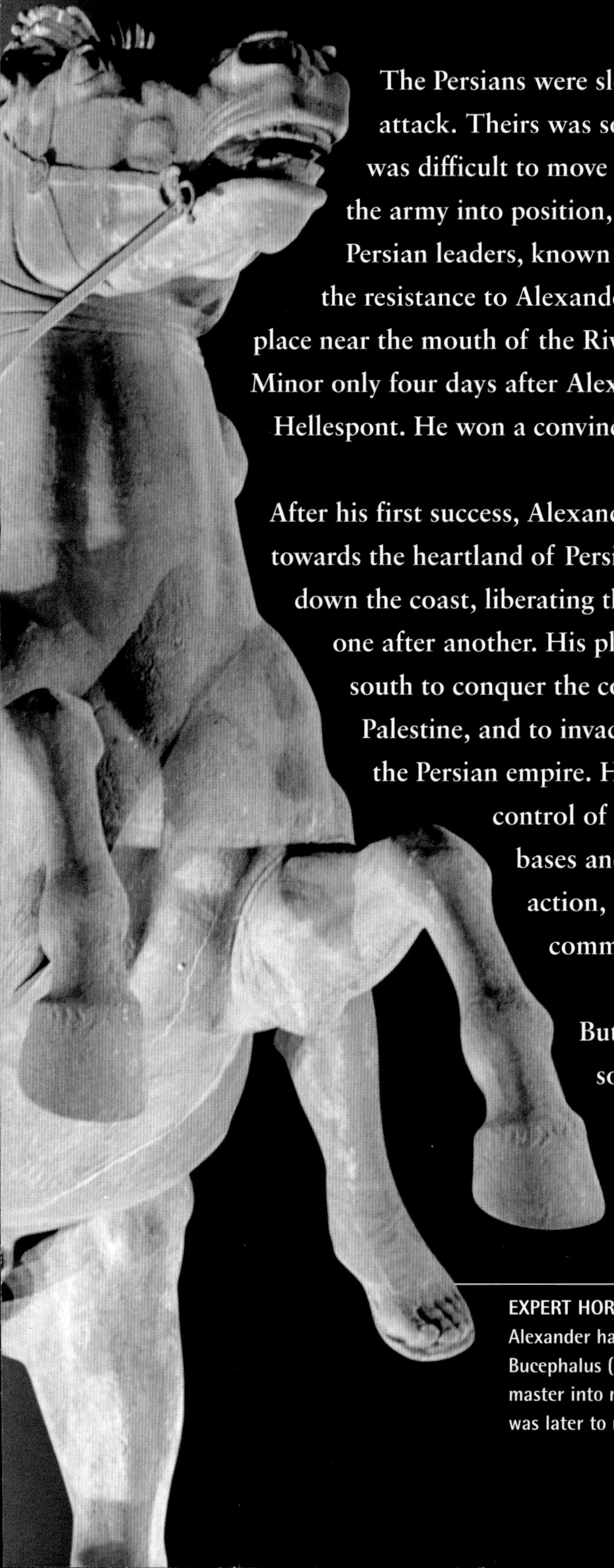

The Persians were slow and hesitant under attack. Theirs was so vast an empire that it was difficult to move the different units of the army into position, and it was left to local Persian leaders, known as satraps, to organize the resistance to Alexander. The first battle took place near the mouth of the River Granicus in Asia Minor only four days after Alexander's crossing of the Hellespont. He won a convincing victory.

After his first success, Alexander did not head towards the heartland of Persia, but turned south down the coast, liberating the Greek cities of Ionia one after another. His plan was to continue south to conquer the coast of Syria and Palestine, and to invade Egypt, also part of the Persian empire. He would thus gain control of all Persia's naval bases and put its fleet out of action, so giving him command of the sea.

But first, according to some stories, he made a detour to the town of Gordium where there was a famous puzzle

HERACLES
Philip of Macedon claimed descent from Heracles, the legendary strongman and son of the god Zeus. Although Heracles was born in Thebes, Alexander came to hate the birthplace of his ancestor and destroyed the city without mercy.

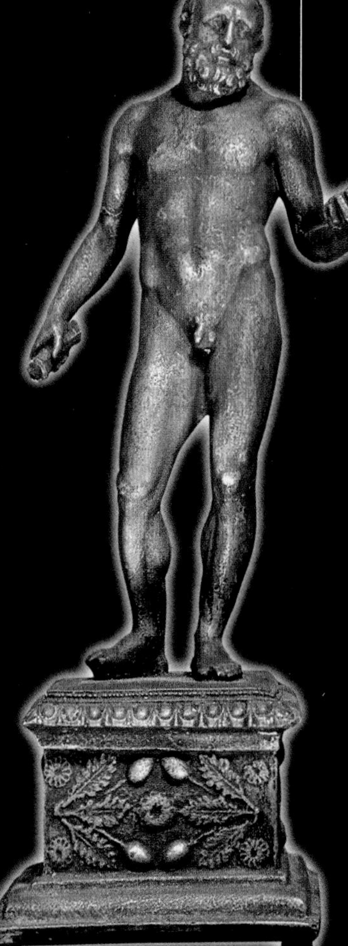

EXPERT HORSEMAN
Alexander had a favourite horse called Bucephalus (Oxhead), who carried his master into many battles. Alexander was later to name a city after him.

called the Gordian knot. It was said that the person who unravelled the knot would become the "lord of all Asia". Alexander did not hesitate. He took out his sword and cut the knot in half. Now the world was all before him. For the next 11 years, he would be continuously fighting a campaign of conquest.

PERSIAN RULERS
This sculpture shows a satrap, the governor of a Persian province. Satraps were appointed by the Persian king and were responsible for collecting taxes and controlling local officials. During the reign of Darius, the number of satraps varied from 20 to 28. To prevent the concentration of power in one man's hands, certain officials, responsible only to the king, checked up on the satraps.

By now the Great King of Persia, Darius III, had gathered his forces and was on Alexander's trail. They met in the north of Syria at a place called Issus. Alexander always shared the danger of the fiercest fighting with his men and never shirked the challenge of battle. He was an obvious target as he wore a brightly coloured cloak, a plumed helmet, and armour that shone in the sun, and he was wounded so often that his body was covered with scars. At the battle of Issus, he made a daring and ferocious attack at the very centre of the Persian army, forcing the Persian king to flee in his chariot.

As a result of this terrible onslaught, Darius abandoned both his army and his family, who by tradition had accompanied him into battle. Now his wife, mother and children were in Alexander's

hands. When Darius offered to make a treaty in order to get them back, Alexander treated him with scorn. "I am the lord of all Asia," he told Darius, "so you must come to me."

GORDIAN KNOT
This painting shows Alexander solving the puzzle of the Gordian knot. It was a rope tied to a wagon in such a complicated way that no one could undo the knot. Alexander solved the problem by cutting through the knot with his sword.

But Alexander did not pursue Darius. He kept to his plan of marching south. Tyre, the greatest of the Mediterranean coastal cities, resisted him for eight months before he took it by storm. He showed no mercy when it fell, killing and enslaving many thousands of people. Now he continued on almost without a struggle, and when he reached Egypt, the Persian satrap surrendered at once to the invading conqueror. The Egyptians hated being under Persian rule and welcomed Alexander as a liberator. Alexander spent six months in Egypt, and greatly pleased the Egyptians by honouring their gods and following their

ETERNAL FAME
This mosaic shows Alexander about to charge into the Battle of Issus. Alexander's personal motive for the attack on the Persians was to prove he was an even greater conqueror than his father.

ancient customs. He visited the Oracle of Amun in the desert at Siwa. Amun was the great god of the Egyptians, just as Zeus was the great god of the Greeks. When the priests of the oracle hailed him as the "son of Amun", it made a deep impression on Alexander, who had always felt that he was no ordinary human being. As if to confirm this success, Alexander took the title of the great pharaoh, or king, of Egypt, the latest in the long line of rulers that stretched back to the

Alexandria

When Alexander was in Egypt, he made plans to build a great port on the Mediterranean. He chose the site himself and named the city Alexandria. According to one story, he scattered barley on the ground to mark out a plan of the city's streets, but was alarmed when the grain was eaten by birds. However, Aristander, a wise man who was part of the king's entourage, told him it was a good omen because it meant the city would attract many settlers. He was proved to be right. Under Alexander's successors, Alexandria grew to become the greatest city of the Greek world, overtaking even Athens. It survives to this day as the leading port of Egypt, though almost nothing of Alexander's city remains above ground.

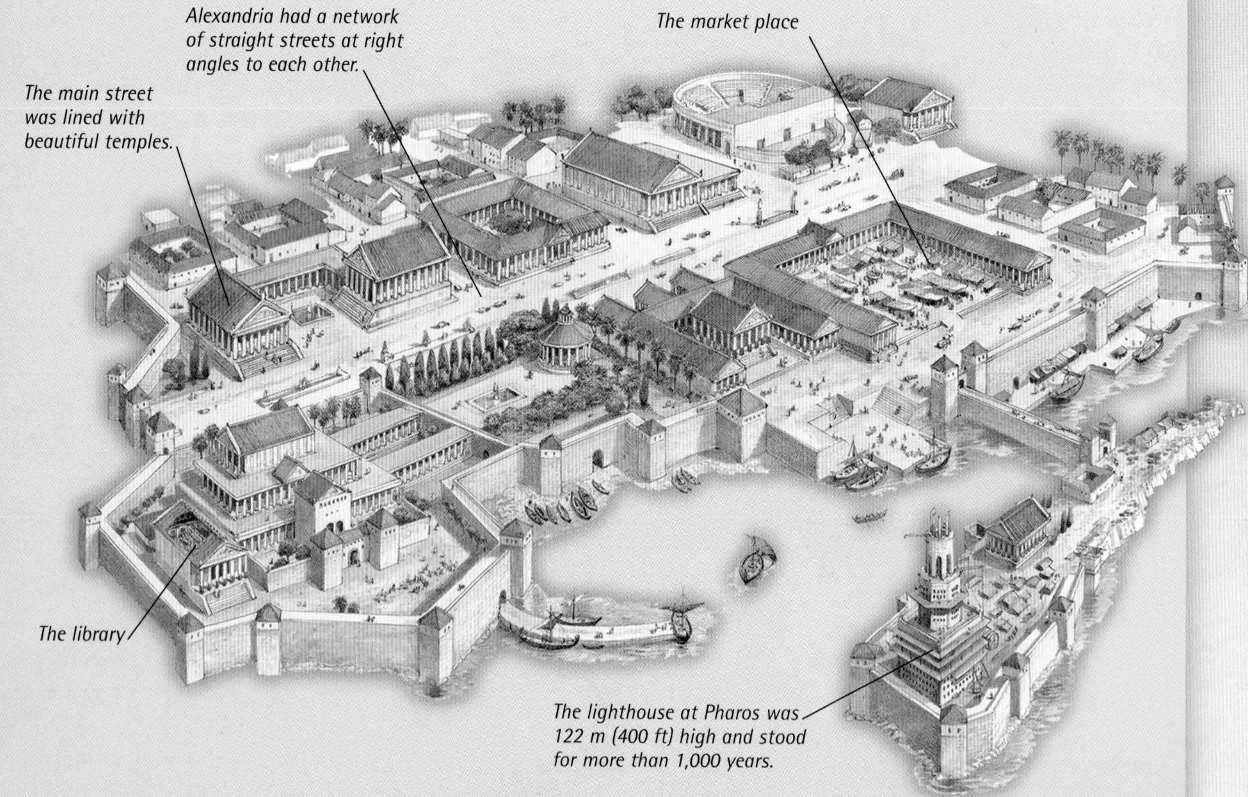

DEATH OF STATIRA
Darius's wife Statira died in childbirth soon after Alexander took the royal family prisoner. Alexander later married her eldest daughter, also named Statira.

beginning of Egyptian history and included Tutenkhamun and Ramesses II. While he was in Egypt, Alexander founded a new city called Alexandria. It would later become the greatest city of the Greek world.

The time had now come to confront Darius, the Great King of Persia, once more. So Alexander marched east towards Persia, and the two armies came face to face at a place called Gaugamela, near the border of modern Iran and Iraq. Once more, Alexander and his warriors charged the central body of the Persians, and once more, Darius took flight. Alexander was proclaimed king of Asia by his men and marched on through the lands of Persia.

Next, Alexander captured the ancient city of Babylon, once the centre of a great empire that had been conquered by the Persians. He seized the royal treasury at Susa and then went on to conquer Persepolis, the royal capital and sacred city of the Persians. He gave his men permission to loot its rich palaces and temples, and then burnt its buildings to the ground in order to prove that he now held the Persian empire's destiny in his hands.

With Persepolis in ruins, Alexander set off in pursuit of Darius. Meanwhile, Darius's satraps had lost faith in his leadership and plotted to overthrow him. Before Alexander could reach Darius, messengers brought news that the Persian king had been captured and killed by his own men. Alexander treated Darius with all the

AMUN
Egyptian priests greeted Alexander as the son of Amun, the chief god of the Egyptians. This carving shows Amun, wearing a crown of goose feathers, seated next to his companion, the goddess Mut.

ALEXANDER'S JOURNEY
Alexander left Pella, the capital of Macedon, in 334 BCE. Within ten years he had conquered territory as far as India. This map shows his route.

honours due to a fallen king. His body was taken back for burial in the rock tombs of the Persian kings, near Persepolis. By honouring his dead rival this way, Alexander reinforced his own claim to be king of Persia.

Now that King Darius was dead, Alexander was not only the most powerful man in the world, but he was also the ruler of the world's wealthiest empire. At this

INVADER OF INDIA
Alexander won a great battle against an Indian king called Poros, whose huge army included more than 100 elephants. In this painting, Alexander, in his red battle cloak, accepts Poros's surrender.

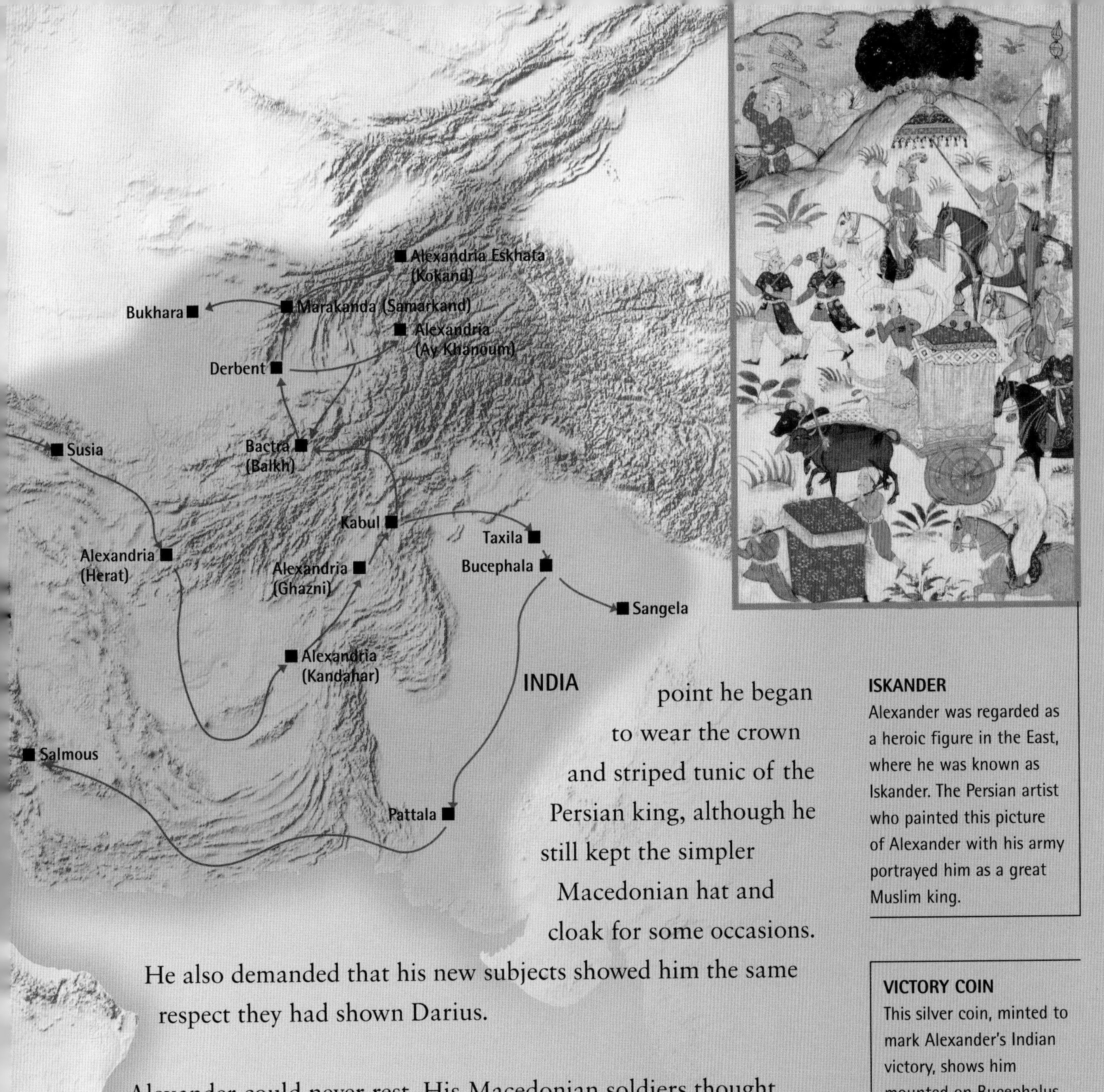

point he began to wear the crown and striped tunic of the Persian king, although he still kept the simpler Macedonian hat and cloak for some occasions. He also demanded that his new subjects showed him the same respect they had shown Darius.

Alexander could never rest. His Macedonian soldiers thought that now the war was over they could go home, but Alexander had different ideas. Instead of enjoying his victory, he decided to keep on marching and conquering. So he journeyed ever deeper into Asia. For three years, he led his army backwards and forwards through the mountains of Uzbekistan and Afghanistan, fighting a series of long campaigns against local tribesmen. And then, in 327 BCE, he crossed into northwest India. Here, beside the River Hydaspes (now known as the Jhelum), he fought and won a battle against an Indian king called Poros.

ISKANDER
Alexander was regarded as a heroic figure in the East, where he was known as Iskander. The Persian artist who painted this picture of Alexander with his army portrayed him as a great Muslim king.

VICTORY COIN
This silver coin, minted to mark Alexander's Indian victory, shows him mounted on Bucephalus attacking King Poros, who is riding an elephant.

The Macedonians had no maps or charts for these distant regions. Greek geographers believed that beyond the known world there was only a dark ocean, which no one could cross. But now Alexander heard rumours of more lands to conquer and more riches to win, stretching away far beyond the horizon. He wanted to go on. And this was of course Alexander's true ambition – he wished to be king of the world. But his Macedonian army would no longer follow him. They were far from home, exhausted, and frightened by the tales of monsters and enchantments that lay ahead of them. In addition, their horses could not abide the smells or noises of the Indian elephants. Alexander tried to persuade his troops onwards, but they refused. So, for the first time in his life, he had to stop. He saved face by saying that the omens were not favourable.

So, in the summer of 325 BCE, Alexander the Great left India to return to Persia.

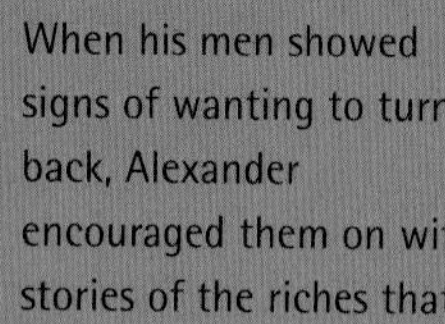

RICHES OF THE EAST
When his men showed signs of wanting to turn back, Alexander encouraged them on with stories of the riches that lay ahead. He ordered his men not to kill animals and birds they had not seen before, including peacocks. Instead, he sent the feathers back to Greece.

ORACLE AT SIWA
This photograph shows the ruins of Amun's shrine at Siwa in Egypt. Although Alexander expressed a wish to be buried here, no one is sure of the actual site of his grave.

Their terrible journey took them through the burning deserts of southern Iran. More soldiers perished from hunger and thirst during the desert crossing than had died in all the battles in Asia. But, at last, Alexander got back to Babylon. He and his Macedonians had been away from home for 10 years.

Ever since his encounter with the oracle at Siwa, Alexander felt himself to be no ordinary man, and now he began to behave as if he were a god. It is perhaps not surprising, considering how much he had achieved. Alexander had spent almost all of his 13-year reign at war. In the process, he destroyed for ever the power of the Greek city-states. But there is a curious irony here. Wherever he went on his campaigns through Asia, he created city-states on the Greek model. At least 13 of them were called Alexandria in his honour, and he is said to have founded some 70 cities altogether. He peopled them with Macedonian and Greek soldiers, and these cities helped to spread the idea of Greek civilization throughout western Asia. The culture and the reputation of the Greeks survived in the world largely through Alexander's efforts. In some ways, that was to be his most enduring legacy.

FAMOUS FACE
In the course of his reign, Alexander issued huge quantities of coins bearing his portrait. Because he conquered such a vast empire, his distinctive face was known throughout the ancient world, from Egypt as far as India.

CHAPTER ELEVEN

The legacy of Greece

In 323 BCE, Alexander died of a fever in Babylon at the age of 32. He had conquered the greatest empire the world had ever seen, but it was too vast to be ruled by any one man. In the absence of a strong heir, Alexander's generals fought for power.

ALEXANDER HAD MARRIED a Persian princess named Roxane, and their child, a son, was born after his father's death. Alexander also had a half-brother called Arrhidaeus. However, none of Alexander's relatives had the opportunity to rule – his wife, mother, son and half-brother were all murdered in the power struggle that followed his death. With no obvious successor, his generals fought one another for a share of the empire, and by 281 BCE, three separate kingdoms had emerged, each ruled by a single dynasty or family.

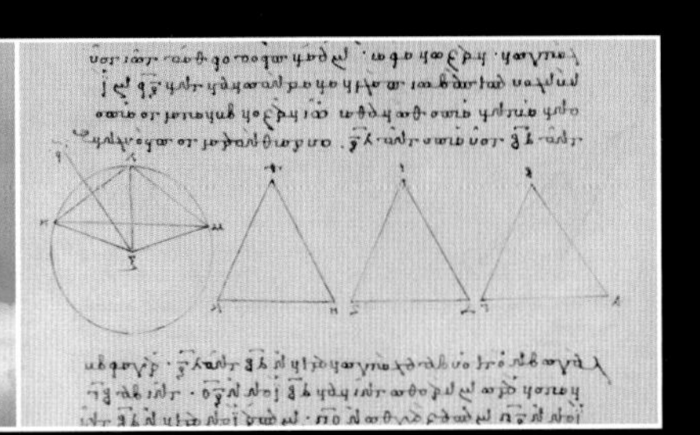

The largest territory was seized by Seleucus, an ambitious general, who was nicknamed "the conqueror". The Seleucid empire covered a large area that included much of modern Turkey, Iraq, Syria and Iran. A general named Ptolemy took charge of Egypt, where his descendants, the

◀ View of the Temple of Apollo at Corinth

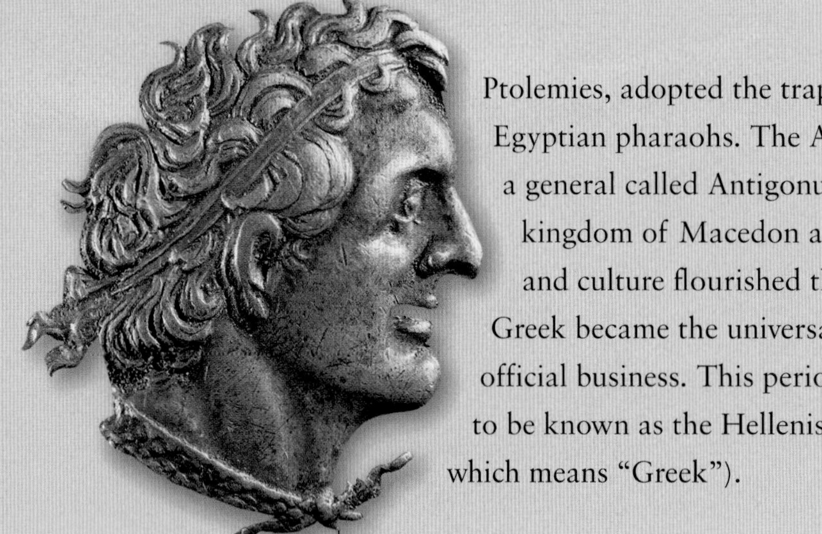

Ptolemies, adopted the trappings and titles of the ancient Egyptian pharaohs. The Antigonids, the dynasty founded by a general called Antigonus, were left with Alexander's own kingdom of Macedon and northern Greece. Greek customs and culture flourished throughout all these kingdoms, and Greek became the universal language of government and official business. This period after Alexander's death has come to be known as the Hellenistic Age (from the word *Hellene*, which means "Greek").

TOUGH SURVIVOR
Ptolemy rose through the ranks of the Macedonian army to become a troop commander. He took control of Egypt after Alexander's death and founded the last dynasty of the pharaohs, known as the Ptolemies, who ruled Egypt from 305 to 30 BCE.

Meanwhile, many of the Greek cities took advantage of the confusion following Alexander's death to rise up in revolt against the Macedonians. Ever since the reign of Philip, the Greek city-states had been forced to join the League of Corinth under Macedonian control. Led by Athens, the Greek cities began what was known as the Hellenic War. It lasted for only a short time, and the Athenians suffered a great defeat. Their leaders were executed, and their democracy abolished. From this time forward, the city was administered by oligarchs, and became simply part of the larger Hellenistic

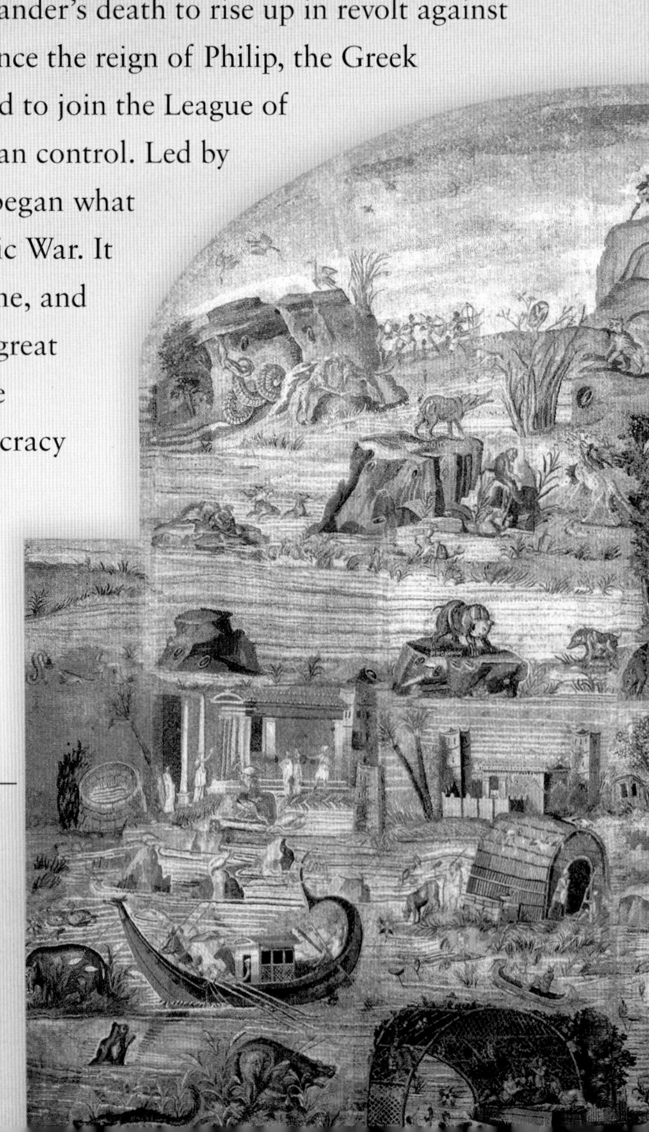

SCENE OF THE NILE
This mosaic shows a glimpse of the bustling life of Egypt in the age of the Ptolemies. The River Nile winds it way through a landscape dotted with crocodiles, lions and hippos to a shore crowded with temples and palaces.

world. After the Hellenic War, the city-states continued to be ruled by Macedonian kings (descendants of the three generals). There were occasional revolts and rebellions from Athens and Sparta, but they were soon put down. To win future support, the kings would endow the cities with temples, walls and other buildings, or send them supplies of corn and timber. But the influence of the once democratic Athens did not come to an end. Its history had been too glorious, and its culture too important, to drift into insignificance. During the Hellenistic Age, Athenian drama flourished, and its schools of philosophy continued to dominate Greek thought.

THE CONQUEROR
Seleucus, who was governor of Babylonia at the time of Alexander's death, fought off his rivals to seize the largest part of Alexander's empire in Asia. He was on his way to Macedon to add to his conquest when he was murdered in 281 BCE.

In Athens, in the 3rd century BCE, there emerged two very different groups of philosophers, known as the Stoics and the Epicureans. Zeno, the founder of the Stoics, used to lecture in the *stoa*, or colonnade, of the Athenian market-place, which is how his followers gained their name. The Stoics believed that virtue was the goal of human life, and that it was achieved through endurance and self-control. All forms of unhappiness and misfortune, as well as strokes of good fortune, should be met calmly, and death itself should hold no terrors for the rational person.

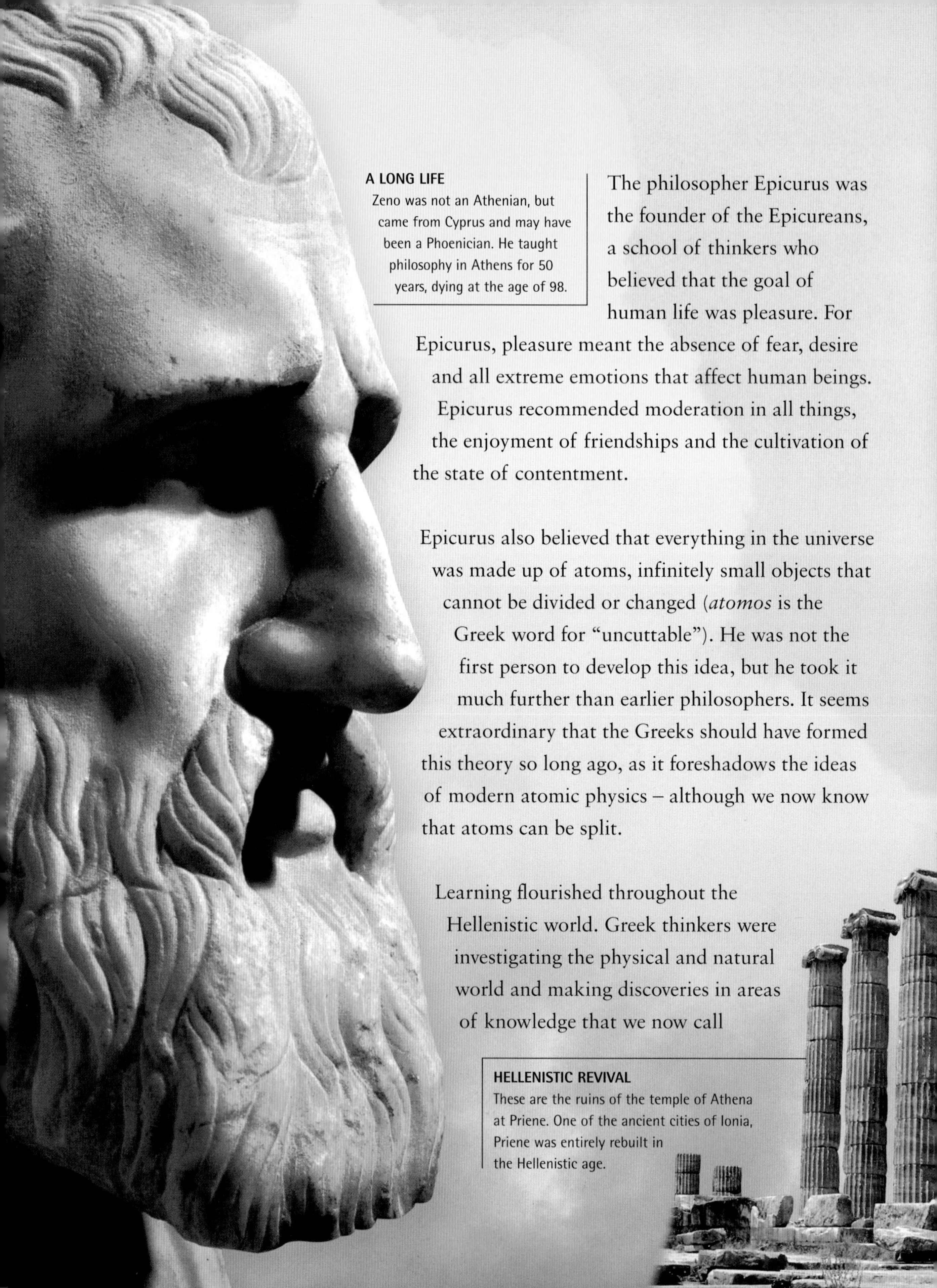

A LONG LIFE
Zeno was not an Athenian, but came from Cyprus and may have been a Phoenician. He taught philosophy in Athens for 50 years, dying at the age of 98.

The philosopher Epicurus was the founder of the Epicureans, a school of thinkers who believed that the goal of human life was pleasure. For Epicurus, pleasure meant the absence of fear, desire and all extreme emotions that affect human beings. Epicurus recommended moderation in all things, the enjoyment of friendships and the cultivation of the state of contentment.

Epicurus also believed that everything in the universe was made up of atoms, infinitely small objects that cannot be divided or changed (*atomos* is the Greek word for "uncuttable"). He was not the first person to develop this idea, but he took it much further than earlier philosophers. It seems extraordinary that the Greeks should have formed this theory so long ago, as it foreshadows the ideas of modern atomic physics – although we now know that atoms can be split.

Learning flourished throughout the Hellenistic world. Greek thinkers were investigating the physical and natural world and making discoveries in areas of knowledge that we now call

HELLENISTIC REVIVAL
These are the ruins of the temple of Athena at Priene. One of the ancient cities of Ionia, Priene was entirely rebuilt in the Hellenistic age.

science. Scholars studied geometry and arithmetic, as well as geography, astronomy and engineering. One Greek mathematician, Eratosthenes, calculated the circumference of the Earth to a very high degree of accuracy. Astronomers observed the orbiting of the planets and attempted to explain their movements but – following Aristotle – they believed that the Earth was the centre of the universe. When a Greek astronomer, Aristarchos of Samos, suggested that the Earth revolved on its axis and travelled in a circle around the Sun, he was ignored. It was not until the 15th century CE that he was proved correct.

Two of the greatest names in the history of science, Euclid and Archimedes, lived and worked during the Hellenistic Age. Euclid, who lived in Alexandria at the end of the 3rd century BCE, opened new horizons for geometry (the branch of mathematics that deals with the relationships between points, lines, angles, surfaces and solids) with his understanding of three-dimensional spaces. His greatest work was a book called *Elements*, which remained a standard textbook in schools throughout the western world until the beginning of the 20th century.

GARDEN PHILOSOPHER
Epicurus's school in Athens was called "the Garden". Epicurus was unique among Athenian philosophers in allowing women and slaves to listen to his teachings.

ARCHIMEDES' SCREW
This carving shows an Egyptian farmer irrigating his vines by turning a spiral screw to lift water from the Nile. Archimedes is said to have invented this early pumping device.

Archimedes made major discoveries in the fields of mathematics and mechanics. It is Archimedes who is said to have found the solution to a problem when he was stepping into his bath – he had realized that he could calculate the volume of an object by immersing it in water and measuring the volume of the water it displaced. He immediately ran naked into the street crying "Eureka!" which means "I have found it!" Archimedes also demonstrated the power of levers to move great weights and is claimed to have said, "Give me a firm spot on which to stand, and I shall move the Earth."

Greek was the common language of the Hellenistic world, and Greek officials were needed at every level of government and administration in the new courts and capitals of the Hellenistic kings. These rulers were very rich indeed. They displayed their wealth in magnificent new buildings and works of art. Hellenistic sculptures become much larger than those of the Classical Age of the 5th and 4th centuries BCE, and figures were often free-standing instead of being part of a carved frieze. Hellenistic sculptors started to broaden the subject matter of their art. Instead of concentrating on traditional sculptures of gods and goddess, they began to include subjects such as animals, children, the old and the dying. Sculptors tried to portray extremes of

THE TOWER OF WINDS
Sculptures representing different types of winds decorate the eight sides of this tower in Athens, built to house a water clock. The roof of this unusual building supported a weather vane.

emotion in their work, conveying mood through facial expression and posture. It is also interesting that the Greeks began to write novels and biographies at this time, showing a new interest in individual expression.

The cities of the Hellenistic world were built in the style of Athens and the other Greek city-states, with temples and public buildings arranged around the *agora*, or market-place. The most important institution of the new Greek cities in Asia seems to have been the gymnasium, which was a cross between a school and an athletics club. Here the boys and young men of the city were educated and trained to take part in the various festivals and competitions that formed a large part of Greek life. Archaeologists have even found a gymnasium at a place called Ay Khanoum, on the borders of Tajikistan and Afghanistan, more than 4,800 km (3,000 miles) from Greece. Originally a city founded by Alexander (and called Alexandria Oxiana), it was one of the most remote outposts of Greek civilization. Even this far from home, Greeks would find a familiar atmosphere and setting.

The greatest Greek city of the Hellenistic world was Alexandria, on the coast of Egypt. This was the first city founded by Alexander, and the first one to which he gave his name. Although the

EUCLID'S BOOK
This is a page from Euclid's *Elements*, a 13-volume work on geometry. In his book, Euclid also summed up the teachings of mathematicians who had lived before him.

THE DYING GAUL
This famous statue called *The Dying Gaul* is a marble copy of a bronze original, now lost. It was made for the ruler of the Hellenistic kingdom of Pergamon in Asia Minor in the mid 3rd century BCE. It shows a vanquished barbarian, his head bowed in defeat.

LEGENDARY QUEEN
This coin bears the image of the most famous Hellenistic monarch – Queen Cleopatra of Egypt, famed for her beauty and her intelligence.

HORSE AND JOCKEY
Hellenistic artists introduced greater realism than earlier sculptors. This bronze statue was found at the bottom of the sea, where it had been lost in an ancient shipwreck.

Ptolemies ruled in Egypt as pharaohs, they never forgot their Macedonian Greek origins. They made Alexandria their capital, and people from all over the Greek world came to live there. The Ptolemies enriched Alexandria with many fine buildings and monuments, including the Pharos, or lighthouse, which was more than 130 m (440 ft) high and was one of the Seven Wonders of the ancient world. It was built in 279 BCE and stood in Alexandria for more than a thousand years.

The most important building in Alexandria was a library that was thought to contain every book ever written in Greek – it was said that every ship that entered the harbour of Alexandria was searched for books to add to the library's collection. Next to this library was a building where scholars and scientists could study. It was called the Museum, or "the place of the Muses" (the nine Muses were the goddesses of the arts and sciences). Through its library and museum, Alexandria came to rival Athens as a centre of Greek learning in the Hellenistic Age. The mathematician Euclid taught there, and Eratosthenes, who measured the circumference of the world, was head of its great library.

The Hellenistic Age lasted for nearly two

TRAINING GROUND
The wrestling ground at Salamis in Cyprus was the central courtyard of a vast domed gymnasium first built in Hellenistic times, but later extended by the Romans.

centuries before the Romans marched into the Greek-speaking world of the eastern Mediterranean and took over one part of Alexander's legacy after another. Macedon fell to them in 148 BCE, and southern Greece, including Athens, surrendered two years later. Finally, in 31 BCE, with the death of Queen Cleopatra (the last of the Ptolemies), Egypt passed into Roman hands.

The Romans eagerly took up the art, architecture, philosophy and literature of the Greeks. They spread Greek ideas and learning throughout their own empire. When the power of Rome came to an end, Greek culture was kept alive by scholars in the east and west and eventually became part the mainstream of European thought. And so, the ideas that originated in a small Greek city-state 2,500 years ago have survived to this day. Aspects of Greek culture such as democracy and classical art are part of our world culture. That is the true legacy of Greece. That is the glory that was Greece.

THE GLORY OF GREECE
This Corinthian column is from the temple of Castor and Pollux in Rome. The Romans were influenced by Hellenistic art and architecture and modelled many of their buildings on Greek designs. The Greeks left a lasting memorial of themselves in stone, and their enduring legacy is still to be seen all around us.

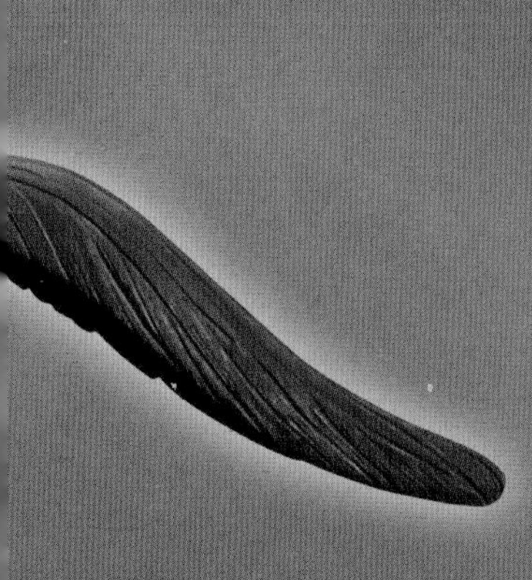

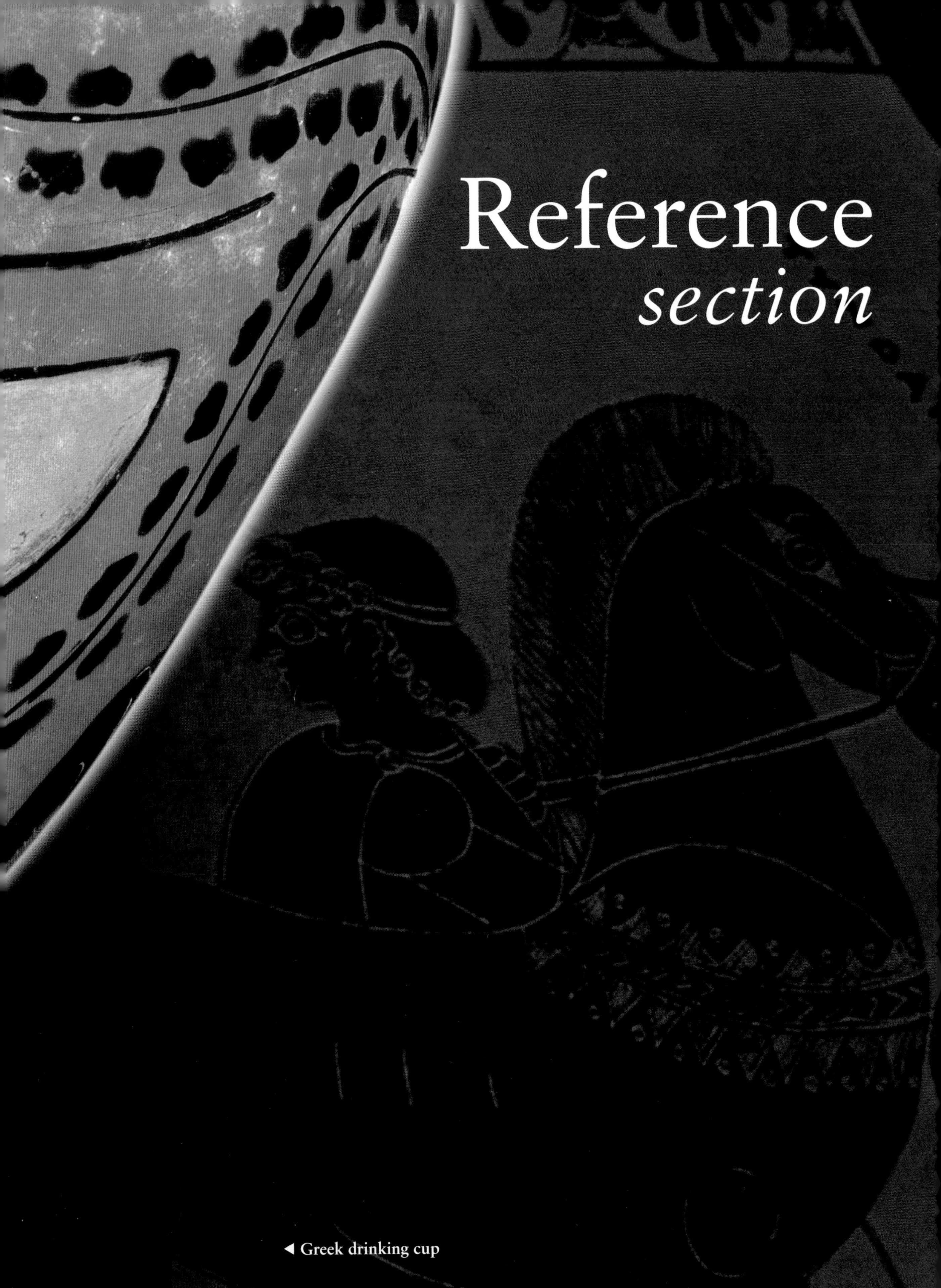

Reference *section*

◄ Greek drinking cup

Clues to the past

ALTHOUGH GREEK CIVILIZATION came to an end more than 2,000 years ago, our knowledge of ancient Greece comes from the variety of artefacts, buildings and everyday items the Greeks left behind. From the archaeological excavations of cities, palaces and tombs, we can build up a picture of life at different periods of Greek history. The works of Greek writers can still be read today, and pottery and frescoes give us a glimpse of everyday life in ancient Greece.

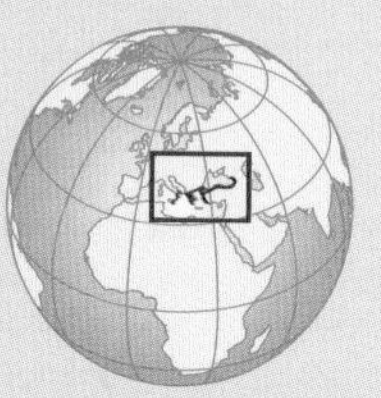

Pottery

Archaeologists have found many examples of Greek pottery from different periods. Many of these pots were decorated with scenes from mythology and everyday life, which provide useful information on the way the ancient Greeks lived. Archaeologists can discover whether a piece of pottery is an ancient original or a modern fake using a technique called thermoluminescence, which reveals the true date of each piece.

Jug with a griffin's head made in the 7th century BCE.

Written evidence

Although few original ancient Greek manuscripts have survived, many Greek writings were copied by hand by the Romans in the 2nd century BCE. Writing found on coins, clay tablets and public monuments provides a valuable insight into the lives of the ancient Greeks, including birth and death dates of rulers, as well as details of battles and major events.

Stone tablets found in a workshop at Olympia.

MACEDONIA
Delphi
Corinth
Olympia
Mycenae
Epidaurus
Ionian Sea
Sparta
Mediterranean Sea

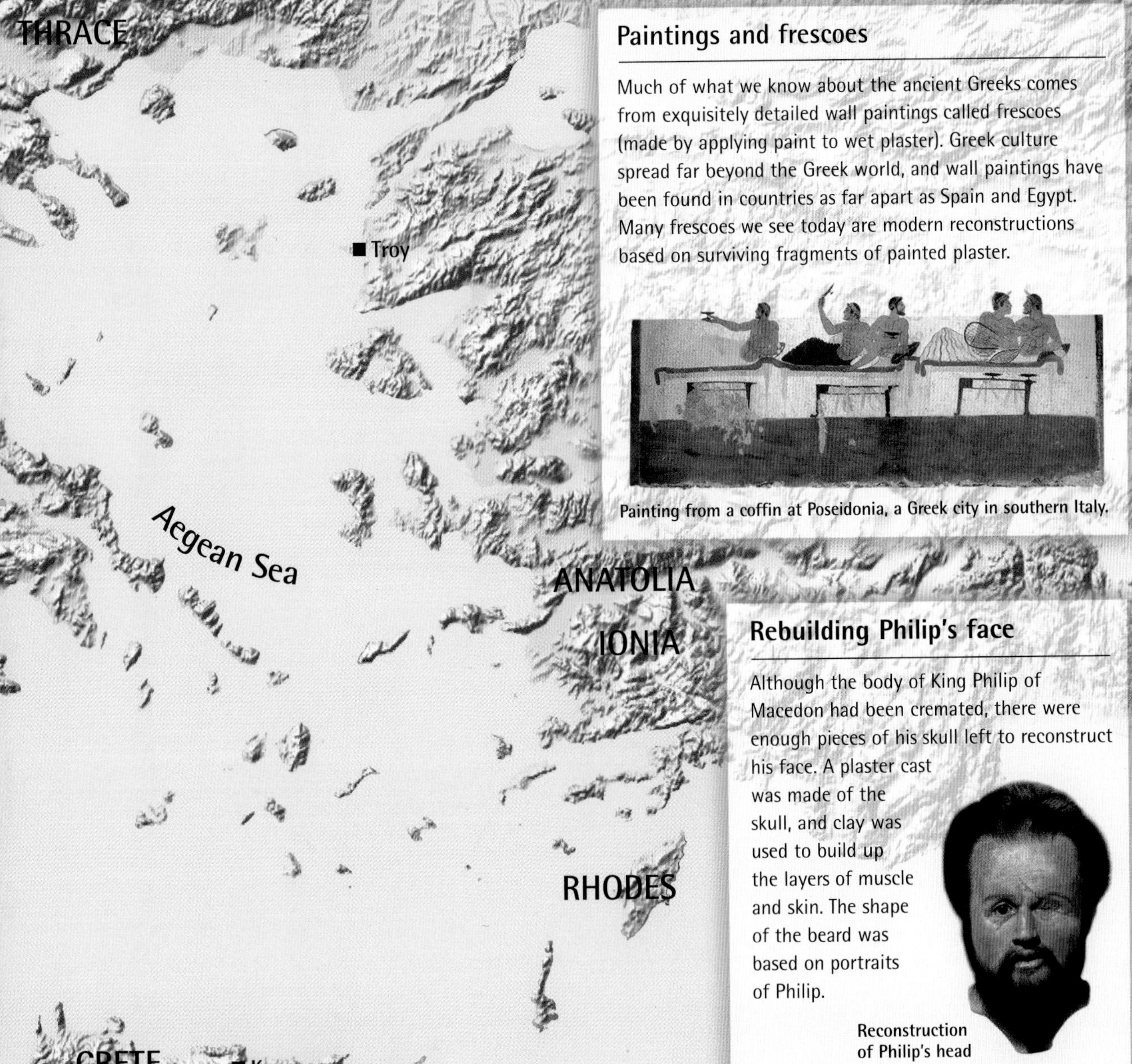

Paintings and frescoes

Much of what we know about the ancient Greeks comes from exquisitely detailed wall paintings called frescoes (made by applying paint to wet plaster). Greek culture spread far beyond the Greek world, and wall paintings have been found in countries as far apart as Spain and Egypt. Many frescoes we see today are modern reconstructions based on surviving fragments of painted plaster.

Painting from a coffin at Poseidonia, a Greek city in southern Italy.

Rebuilding Philip's face

Although the body of King Philip of Macedon had been cremated, there were enough pieces of his skull left to reconstruct his face. A plaster cast was made of the skull, and clay was used to build up the layers of muscle and skin. The shape of the beard was based on portraits of Philip.

Reconstruction of Philip's head

Finding the evidence

Archaeological sites are found during building work, through reading historical documents, by field walking and by carrying out geophysical surveys (studying the soil's structure). Aerial photography can also show the outlines of ancient walls and ditches. Once a suitable site has been identified, a plan is made of the area before digging begins. During a dig, archaeologists make a detailed record of every find. The position in which an artefact is found can tell experts a lot about the age and purpose of the object, as well as the surrounding area.

The palace at Knossos, discovered by British archaeologist Sir Arthur Evans.

The gods

THE GREEKS WORSHIPPED MANY DIFFERENT gods and goddesses, each associated with a different aspect of life or death. They believed that all gods were descendants of Gaia (the earth) and Uranos (the sky). Below is a list of the most important Greek gods and goddesses.

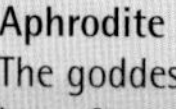

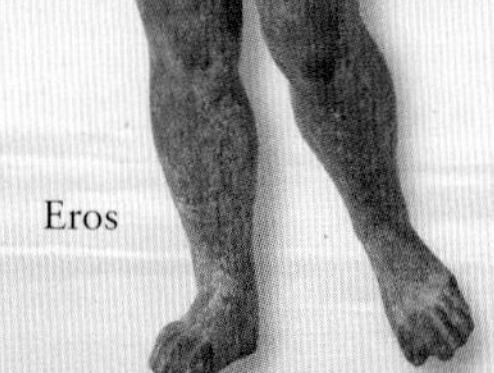

Eros

Aphrodite
The goddess of love was born from the sea foam and was carried by the west winds to Cyprus. Although she was married to Hephaistos, she fell in love with Ares, the god of war.

Apollo
Patron of the arts and the god of the Sun and of healing and medicine. He was the twin brother of the goddess Artemis. His symbol was a laurel tree.

Ares
The god of war was said to have a violent temper. His symbols were a burning torch, a spear, dogs and vultures.

Artemis
The goddess of the Moon and hunting was usually portrayed with a bow and quiver. Her silver arrows brought plague and death, but she also helped women in childbirth. Her symbols were deer and dogs.

Dionysus

Aphrodite

Asclepius
The god of medicine and healing. Many Greeks travelled to his shrines in the hope of a cure.

Athena
The daughter of Zeus, Athena was the goddess of wisdom and war and the patron goddess of Athens. Her symbols were the owl and the olive tree.

Demeter
The goddess of harvests and grain. When her daughter Persephone was kidnapped by Hades, god of the underworld, Demeter abandoned her duties to go in search of her. Her symbol was a sheaf of wheat.

Dionysus
God of wine, drama and fertility, Dionysus was the son of Zeus and of the mortal heroine Semele. He led a wild life of pleasure and indulgence and was attended by a band of merry revellers. He was thought to die each year and be born again in the spring.

Eris
The daughter of Zeus and Hera, Eris was the vengeful goddess of spite and mischief.

Eros
God of love, whose weapons were darts, the tips of which were treated to make people fall in love. He fell in love with the mortal (human) Psyche when he was accidentally grazed with his own arrow.

Hades
Also known as Pluto, Hades was the god of the underworld. He drove a golden chariot and guarded the dead jealously. He kidnapped Persephone to be his wife.

Hebe
Goddess of youth and cup-bearer to the gods. She married the hero Heracles after he was made a god.

Hephaistos
The crippled god Hephaistos was a blacksmith. He was the god of fire and craftworkers and the husband of Aphrodite.

Hera
The mother of Ares, Hera protected marriage and women. Her symbols were the peacock and the pomegranate.

Hermes
This mischievous messenger of the gods wore wings on his sandals and hat and carried a staff. He was the patron of travellers, traders and thieves.

Hestia
Bright, gentle and pure, Hestia was the goddess of the hearth and home. Every Greek family had a shrine dedicated to her.

Pan
The son of Hermes, Pan was the god of shepherds and nature. A lover of music, he wandered through the fields and forests playing the pipes.

Persephone
Kidnapped by Hades to be queen of the underworld, she spent half the year (autumn and winter) with Hades and half the year (spring and summer) with her mother. According to legend, this was the origin of the seasons.

Poseidon
King of the sea and god of earthquakes, Poseidon rode a golden chariot and lived in a palace under the water. He carried a three-pronged trident.

Zeus
King of the gods, Zeus controlled the skies and the weather. He married his sister Hera, but was forever unfaithful to her. His symbols were the thunderbolt, the eagle and the oak tree.

Famous people

MORE THAN TWO AND a half thousand years ago, the people of Greece developed one of the most advanced civilizations of the ancient world. The Greeks invented politics, philosophy, drama and the study of history. Listed below are some of the most famous people in the Greek world.

Hippocrates

Aeschylus
(525–456 BCE) Athenian tragic dramatist. His most famous work is the trilogy *Oresteia*, which tells the story of King Agamemnon.

Anaxagoras
(500–428 BCE) Early Greek philosopher who was the first person to explain a solar eclipse.

Archimedes
(c.287–212 BCE) Mathematician, who invented a device for pumping water and a type of pulley for lifting objects.

Aristophanes
(c.450–c.385 BCE) Comic playwright, whose works include *The Wasps*, *The Birds* and *The Frogs*.

Aristotle
(384–322 BCE) Philosopher who founded a school called the Lyceum. He is said to have invented many of the natural sciences.

Aristotle

Demosthenes
(384–322 BCE) Athenian statesman and orator. He is famous for his powerful speeches called the *Philippics*, which criticized King Philip II.

Euripides
(c.485–406 BCE) Tragic playwright. His most famous works include *Bacchae* and *Electra*.

Herodotus
(c.490–c.425 BCE) Historian and author of an account of the Persian Wars.

Euripides

Hippocrates
(c.460–c.370 BCE) Known as "the father of medicine", Hippocrates based his medical practice on observing his patients and their symptoms. He believed there was a rational explanation for all illnesses.

Homer
(8th century BCE) A poet whose most famous works, the *Iliad* and the *Odyssey*, were written down centuries after his death.

Myron
(5th century BCE) Athenian sculptor whose most famous works include a statue of the goddess Athena and the *Discobolos* (discus-thrower).

Pindar
(c.522–c.443 BCE) Regarded as one of the greatest Greek poets, his odes celebrated great leaders and sporting victories.

Plato
(427–347 BCE) Athenian philosopher and pupil of Socrates, Plato set up a school known as the Academy. He set out his theories on how to rule an "ideal" state in his book *The Republic*.

Pythagoras
(c.580–c.500 BCE) Philosopher, mathematician and mystic who led a band of devoted followers in Italy. He is most famous for his work on right-angled triangles.

Sappho
(c.610–c.650 BCE) One of the few known female poets of the ancient world. Sappho wrote about love, family and friends and is known for her lyrical and emotional style.

Socrates
(469–399 BCE) Athenian philosopher and tutor of Plato. He questioned accepted beliefs and was concerned with human ethics.

Sophocles
(c.496–c.405 BCE) Tragic playwright whose most famous works include *Antigone* and *Oedipus Rex*.

Thales
(c.640–c.558 BCE) The first known Greek philosopher, born in Miletus. He believed that the whole universe was derived from water.

Thucydides
(c.460–c.400 BCE) One of the first true historians, he wrote an account of the Peloponnesian War.

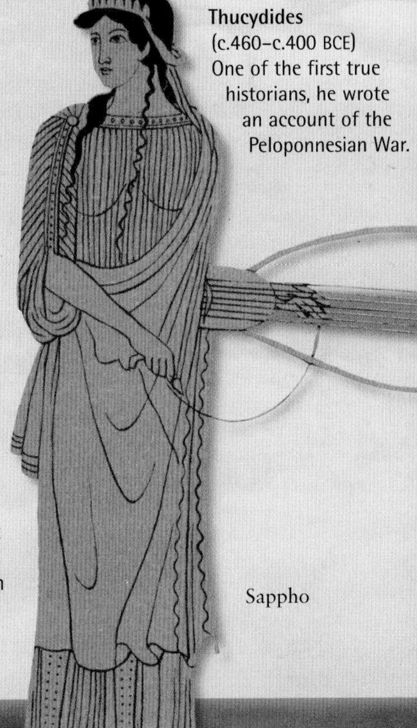
Sappho

Buildings and architecture

THE LASTING INFLUENCE of Greek architecture can be seen in the public buildings of every capital city of the world. Architects in classical Greece followed three main orders or styles – the Doric, Ionic and Corinthian. The proportions and number of columns of Greek buildings were carefully calculated to give an impression of balance and elegance.

Erectheum Temple, Athens

Ionic

The Ionic column was slender and elegant and was popular in eastern Greece and the Greek islands. Its capital was decorated with twin scrolls on either side.

Corinthian

The top (capital) of a Corinthian column was very elaborate and was usually decorated with leaves from the acanthus plant. A pair of scrolls decorated each corner, so that the capital looked the same from all sides. Although the Greeks originated the Corinthian style, it became much more popular with the Romans, who used and adapted Corinthian columns in many of their own buildings.

Temple of Castor and Pollux, Rome

Doric

The Doric style was the most popular in mainland Greece and in the colonies in southern Italy and Sicily. Doric columns were thick, with fluted vertical grooves and no bases. They were crowned with plain, undecorated capitals. The overall effect of the Doric style was strong and powerful.

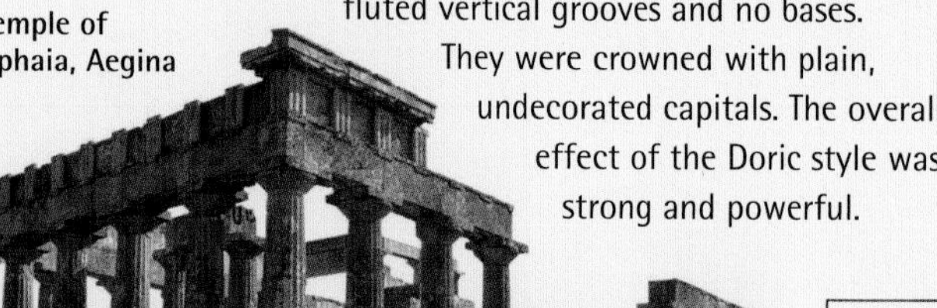

Temple of Aphaia, Aegina

Pediment from the Archaeological Museum, Corfu

Pediments

Most Greek temples were rectangular in shape with a pediment (triangular gable) at each end of the building. The pediment would be carved with sculptures, which were painted in rich shades of red and blue. Brightly coloured glass was used for eyes, and details such as jewels and weapons were made of bronze.

Friezes

Friezes were decorative panels that went all the way round a building in a continuous band. They were carved with panels of sculpture called metopes. Many friezes were used to record events or tell a story. The marble frieze here shows part of the procession of worshippers who came to the Acropolis every four years in honour of the goddess Athena.

Section of the frieze from the Parthenon, Athens

The Doric temple of Poseidon at Sounion

Capital of an Ionic column

Capitals

Ionic columns were decorated with twin spiral designs on either side of the capitals. These spirals, or scrolls, were known as volutes. This Ionic capital features a narrow band of stone at the top, scrolled edging and a decorated band carved with an egg and dart design.

Glossary

Words in *italics* have their own entry in the glossary.

A

Acropolis A citadel or hilltop fortress within a Greek city. The most famous acropolis is that of Athens. *Acropolis* literally means "high city".

Agora An open area in a Greek city used as a market place, administrative centre and public square.

Amphora (plural: *amphorae*) A narrow-necked, two-handled vessel, used for transporting and storing olive oil, wine or water.

Archaic period The period (from about 800–500 BCE) between the *Dark Age* and the *Classical period*.

Archon An Athenian official. Archons were very powerful during the *Archaic period*. During the *Classical period*, their role was mainly ceremonial.

Aristocrat A member of a rich, land-owning family. Aristocrats ruled the *city-states* in the *Archaic period*.

Asia Minor The historical name for Anatolia, the Asian part of Turkey, between the Black Sea, the Aegean and the Mediterranean.

Assembly The main governing body in a Greek *democracy*.

Attica The state of Athens and the surrounding countryside. Most Athenian *citizens* lived in Attica.

B

Barbarian The Greek term for any foreigner who did not speak Greek.

Black-figure A style of pottery made in Athens. It was decorated with black figures on a red background.

Bronze Age The period from about 3000–1100 BCE, when bronze (a mixture of copper and tin) was the principal metal used for making tools.

C

Capital The top part of a column.

Caryatid A statue of a young woman used in place of a column. Caryatids were often used in *Ionic* buildings,

Cella The central hall of a Greek temple.

Centaur A mythological creature with the head and upper body of a man and the lower body of a horse.

Chiton A woman's dress, usually made from one or two pieces of cloth and fastened at the shoulders.

Chorus A group of men in a Greek play, who spoke, sang and danced together. They often commented on the play's action or characters.

Citizen An adult, native-born member of a Greek *city-state*.

City-state A city, which together with the surrounding region, formed an independent state.

Classical period The period from about 480 BCE (the Persian Wars) to about 323 BCE (the death of Alexander the Great). It was a time of great achievements in art and sculpture.

Corinthian One of the orders of Greek architecture. The *capitals* of Corinthian columns were ornately decorated with leaves.

Cuirass Breastplate or armour for the upper part of the body, generally the breast, back and stomach.

D

Dark Age This period in Greek history, which dates from 1100 BCE to about 800 BCE.

Delian League An alliance of Greek states set up by Athens in about 478 BCE to fight the Persians. It was formed on the island of Delos.

Democracy A state or country that is ruled by its people. Athens was the most famous democratic state.

Dorians A Greek tribe, who were the last invaders to arrive in the Greek *peninsula*. They settled mainly in the *Peloponnese* and the southern Aegean islands.

Doric One of the orders of Greek architecture. Doric columns had plain, undecorated *capitals*.

Dynasty A series of kings or rulers from the same family.

E

Electrum A naturally occuring metal made of gold and silver, which was used to make the first coins.

Ephor A Spartan official. Five *ephors* were elected each year to oversee the running of the state.

F

Flutes The vertical channels carved in the shafts of Greek columns.

Fresco A wall painting made by applying wet paint to plaster. The earliest known Greek frescoes were found at the palace at Knossos.

Frieze A horizontal band on a Greek temple, usually decorated with carvings.

G

Geometric The period from about 1050 to about 700 BCE. The term is also used to describe pottery made during this period.

Great Dionysia The main Athenian festival in honour of Dionysus. It was held over a period of five days.

Greave Bronze armour or guard used by Greek *hoplites* to protect the lower leg and shin.

Gymnasium (plural: *gymnasia*) A sports centre including such features as a running track, bathrooms and changing rooms. Many *gymnasia* also had lecture halls and libraries.

H

Hellenistic A term used for the period of Greece following the *Classical period*, from the conquests of Alexander the Great (336–323 BCE) until the Roman conquest of Greece (about 300–150 BCE).

Helot A Spartan slave. Helots were carefully controlled by their masters, who were constantly prepared for rebellion.

Hetaira (plural: *hetairai*) A woman who entertained at parties by singing, dancing or playing music.

Hoplite A heavily armed soldier who fought on foot. Hoplites fought in tight formation with long spears and round shields.

Hydra A jar in which water was fetched from a fountain.

I

Ionic One of the orders of Greek architecture. Ionic columns were decorated with a spiral pattern called a *volute*.

J

Javelin A throwing spear, used in sport and warfare.

K

Krater A large vase for mixing wine with water.

L

Labyrinth A mythical underground maze at the palace at Knossos, where a monster called the minotaur lived.

Libation A drink offering to a god, generally poured over an altar.

Linear A An early form of writing used by the *Minoans*.

Linear B A form of writing composed of signs and pictures used by the *Mycenaeans*.

M

Macedonia A state ruled by Greek kings in the north of Greece.

Magna Graecia A general term for the Greek states of southern Italy.

Megaron A large hall used by the kings in a *Mycenaean* palace.

Metic A free man living in Athens, who did not have the rights of a *citizen*. He had to pay taxes and serve in the army, but he could not vote or own property.

Metope A stone panel on a *frieze*, usually decorated with sculptures.

Minoan An early civilization on the island of Crete. The Minoans were named after the legendary Cretan king, Minos.

Minotaur The legendary bull-headed monster who lived in the palace at Knossos in Crete.

Mosaic A design or picture made of small pieces of glass or stone.

Muses The goddesses (usually nine in number) who acted as patrons of poetry, literature, music and dance.

Mycenaean A civilization on mainland Greece. The Mycenaeans were named after the city of Mycenae, where evidence of their culture was first discovered.

O

Oligarchy A political system in which the few rule over the many. Oligarchs were opposed to *democracy*.

Omen A sign or warning from the gods. Specially trained priests interpreted omens from the intestines of sacrificed animals.

Oracle A god's reply to a worshipper's question or the sacred site where that reply was given. The most famous oracle was the Oracle of Apollo at Delphi.

Orchestra The circular area at the centre of a Greek theatre. The word *orchestra* literally meant "dancing floor" in Greek.

Ostracism A system in which the *citizens* of Athens could vote to banish unpopular politicians. The voters wrote the names of their chosen politicians on *ostraka*, pieces of broken pottery. If 6,000 votes were counted, the politician with the most votes against him was banished from Athens for ten years.

Ostrakon (plural: *ostraka)* A fragment of pottery on which Athenian *citizens* wrote the name of a politician they wanted to see banished.

P

Palaistra A wrestling ground that formed part of the *gymnasium*.

Pankration A combat event in Greek sporting contests. It was a type of wrestling match in which contestants could use any method to defeat their opponent except for biting and eye-gouging. The contest continued until one party surrendered.

Pediment The triangular part in the gables (front and back) of a building. In *Doric* buildings, the pediment was usually decorated with sculptures.

Peloponnese The large landmass that forms the southern part of mainland Greece.

Peninsula An area of land almost surrounded by sea.

Pentathlon An athletic event in the Olympic Games, which comprised five events: jumping, discus-throwing, javelin-throwing, running and wrestling.

Periokoi Descendants of the people who surrendered to Sparta. The word literally means "those who dwell around".

Peristyle A row of columns surrounding a building or courtyard.

Phoenicians A trading people who lived on the coast of present-day Lebanon. They devised the alphabet on which the classical Greek one was based.

Polis An independent town or city, extended in the *Classical period* to mean the whole *city-state*.

Pythia The priestess who was the mouthpiece of the god Apollo at the *Oracle* of Delphi.

R

Red-figure A type of pottery with red figures painted on a black background. Such vases were produced in Athens from the 6th century BCE.

Relief A sculpture carved on stone panels. The stone was cut away, allowing the scene to stand out against a flat background.

S

Sacrifice An offering made to a god or goddess. Animals such as goats, sheep, pigs or cows were sacrificed on an open-air altar. Their intestines were examined for *omens*.

Sanctuary A sacred area for religious worship, often enclosed by a fence or wall and containing a temple.

Sarcophagus A coffin, usually made of stone or clay, although early examples were made of wood.

Satyr play A drama in which the *chorus* were dressed to represent *satyrs*.

Satyrs Spirits of the woods and hills. In 5th-century art, they were shown with beards and horses' ears and tails.

Sea People A group of people who migrated around the eastern Mediterranean in about 1190 BCE.

Shaft-graves Early tombs in which the *Mycenaeans* were buried.

Soothsayer A person who was thought to be able to predict the future.

Sophist A teacher who moved from city to city instructing his pupils in the art of public speaking.

Stoa (plural: *stoae*) A long building with walls at the back and sides, but open at the front, where there was a row of columns to support the roof.

Strategos (plural: *strategoi*) An Athenian army commander and political leader. Ten *strategoi* were elected annually to take care of the city's defence.

T

Terracotta A material made of unfired clay, sand and particles of clay that have previously been baked.

Thirty Tyrants A group of pro-Spartan rulers who ruled Athens after its defeat in the Peloponnesian Wars.

Tholos A circular building, usually with a conical roof and with pillars around the outside.

Tripod A three-legged seat or stand. Tripods were frequently awarded as prizes in athletic or musical competitions.

Trireme A warship, which was propelled by three banks of oarsmen and could carry 200 men.

Tyrant A single ruler of a state, who obtained power through popular support or by force of arms.

V

Volute A spiral decoration, usually seen on *Ionic capitals*.

Index

Credits

The publisher would like to thank the following for their kind permission to reproduce their photographs:

(Key: a-above; c-centre; b-below; l-left; r-right; t-top)

1 Corbis: Araldo de Luca. **2** DK Images: Courtesy of the Royal Ontario Museum, Toronto (bl); The British Museum, London (br); The Nicholas P. Goulandris Foundation Museum of Cycladic Art, Athens (c). **3** DK Images: The British Museum, London (bc). Getty Images: Walter Bibikow (bcrr). Scala Art Resource: Galleria Palatina, Florence, Italy (bcr). **6** The Art Archive: (cbr). **7** DK Images: The British Museum, London (clb); Courtesy of the Royal Ontario Museum, Toronto (cb). **8** DK Images: The British Museum, London (bl). **8-9** The Art Archive. **10** akg-images: Erich Lessing (bl). DK Images: The British Museum, London (tl). **11** The Art Archive: Heraklion Museum / Dagli Orti (tr); National Archaeological Museum Athens / Dagli Orti (b). **13** DK Images: The British Museum, London (br). **14** DK Images: The British Museum, London (br); Courtesy of the Royal Ontario Museum, Toronto (bl). **15** akg-images: Erich Lessing (tr). DK Images: The British Museum, London (br). **16** akg-images: Erich Lessing (tl). **16-17** Sonia Halliday Photographs: F.H.C Birch (c). Robert Harding Picture Library: Loraine Wilson (t). **17** akg-images: (tr). **18** Corbis: Roger Wood (cbr). **19** www.bridgeman.co.uk: Bibliotheque des Arts Decoratifs, Paris, France, Archives Charmet (clb). **20** The Art Archive: Bibliothèque des Arts Décoratifs Paris / Dagli Orti (tl). **21** DK Images: The British Museum, London (tr). Science Photo Library: Simon Lewis (br). **22** DK Images: The British Museum, London (tl). The Art Archive: Archaeological Museum Eretria / Dagli Orti (br). **23** Robert Harding Picture Library: John Miller. **24-25** Corbis: Roger Wood (b). **25** DK Images: The British Museum, London (tr). **26** Ancient Art & Architecture Collection: (bl). © Michael Holford: (tr). **27** www.bridgeman.co.uk: Bibliotheque des Arts Decoratifs, Paris, France, Archives Charmet. **28** The Art Archive: Dagli Orti. **29** DK Images: Courtesy of The British Library (clb). **30** DK Images: Courtesy of The British Library (bc); The British Museum, London (bl). The Art Archive: Antiquarium di Santa Severa / Dagli Orti (tl). **30-31** DK Images: Courtesy of The British Library (b). **32** The Art Archive: Bibliothèque des Arts Décoratifs Paris / Dagli Orti (t). **33** akg-images: Nimatallah (tr). www.bridgeman.co.uk: Vatican Museums and Galleries, Vatican City, Italy (br). **34** DK Images: The British Museum, London (b). Robert Harding Picture Library: Charles Bowman (t). **37** DK Images: The British Museum, London (tr). The Art Archive: Dagli Orti (bl). **39** Corbis: Archivo Iconografico, S.A. (tl). DK Images: The British Museum, London (br). **40** The British Museum, London (tl), (br). **40-41** DK Images: Sean Hunter (t). **41** Ancient Art & Architecture Collection: (cr). **42** The Art Archive: Archaeological Museum Naples / Dagli Orti. **43** The Art Archive: National Gallery London / John Webb (cb). **44** DK Images: The British Museum, London (bl), (bc). **45** Ancient Art & Architecture Collection: (b). The Art Archive: National Gallery London / John Webb (tl). **46** DK Images: The British Museum, London (tl). **47** Ancient Art & Architecture Collection: (bl). **48** www.bridgeman.co.uk: Bibliotheque Nationale, Paris, France, Archives Charmet. **49** Ancient Art & Architecture Collection: (bl). www.bridgeman.co.uk: Private Collection, Boltin Picture Library (r). **50** akg-images: Erich Lessing (tr). Ancient Art & Architecture Collection: (l). **51** akg-images: Erich Lessing (b). **52** www.bridgeman.co.uk: Archaeological Museum, Istanbul, Turkey / Giraudon. **54** www.bridgeman.co.uk: Museo Archeologico Nazionale, Naples, Italy (bl). **54-55** akg-images: (b). **57** DK Images: The British Museum, London (tl). **58** DK Images: The British Museum, London (tl). **59** DK Images: The British Museum, London (b). Mary Evans Picture Library: (tl). **60** www.bridgeman.co.uk: House of Masks, Delos, Greece (tl). **60-61** akg-images (c). **61** akg-images: (br). DK Images: The British Museum, London (tr). **62** akg-images: Erich Lessing. **63** Corbis: Araldo de Luca (clb). **64** Corbis: Araldo de Luca (t). **65** DK Images: The British Museum, London (tr). © Michael Holford: (b). **66** akg-images: Eric Lessing (l). **67** Ancient Art & Architecture Collection: (tl). Robert Harding Picture Library: (b). **68** Ancient Art & Architecture Collection: (tl). **68-69** akg-images: Joseph Martin. **71** akg-images: Peter Connolly (tl). **72** www.bridgeman.co.uk: National Museums of Scotland (tl). DK Images: The British Museum, London (br). **73** akg-images: (br). **74** akg-images: Peter Connolly (cbr). The Art Archive: Archaeological Museum Piraeus / Dagli Orti. **76-77** Robert Harding Picture Library: Marco Simoni. **77** www.bridgeman.co.uk: © Museum of Fine Arts, Houston, Texas, USA, Gift of Miss Annette Finnegan (tr). **78** akg-images: Erich Lessing (tl). **78-79** DK Images: The Nicholas P. Goulandris Foundation Museum of Cycladic Art, Athens (c). **79** DK Images: The British Museum, London (tr). **80** The Art Archive: Archaeological Museum Naples / Dagli Orti. **81** akg-images: Erich Lessing (tr); Peter Connolly (b). **82** With permission of the Royal Ontario Museum © ROM (bl). **83** akg-images: Erich Lessing (tr). **84** DK Images: The British Museum, London (l). **84-85** akg-images (bc). **85** DK Images: The British Museum, London (r). **86** akg-images: Erich Lessing (bl). DK Images: The British Museum, London (tr). **87** akg-images: Erich Lessing (tr). **88** DK Images: The British Museum, London (bl). **89** The Art Archive: Bibliothèque des Arts Décoratifs Paris / Dagli Orti (b); Musée du Louvre Paris / Dagli Orti (tr). **90** The Art Archive: Archaeological Museum Venice / Dagli Orti. **91** DK Images: The British Museum, London (cb). **93** DK Images: The British Museum, London (tr), (b). **94** The Art Archive: Archaeological Museum Piraeus / Dagli Orti (l). **95** Corbis: Gianni Dagli Orti (b). **96** DK Images: Courtesy of Alan Meek for armour and weapons (tl). The Art Archive: Kanellopoulos Museum Athens / Dagli Orti (b). **97** akg-images: Erich Lessing (r). **98** www.bridgeman.co.uk: Museo Archeologico Nazionale, Naples, Italy, Alinari. DK Images: NASA (cbr). **99** Scala Art Resource: Galleria Palatina, Florence, Italy (cb). **100** DK Images: NASA (bl). **100-101** Robert Harding Picture Library: PhotoTake. **101** akg-images: Pirozzi (tr). **102-103** Scala Art Resource: Galleria Palatina, Florence, Italy. **104** akg-images: John Hios (bl). **105** The Art Archive: Vatican Museum Rome / Joseph Martin (br). **106** The Art Archive: Archaeological Museum Naples / Dagli Orti. **107** The Art Archive: Victoria and Albert Museum London / Eileen Tweedy (cb). **108** The Art Archive: Collection Antonovich / Dagli Orti (tl). **111** The Art Archive: Archaeological Museum Salonica / Dagli Orti (tr). Kostas Kontos: (br). **112-113** Getty Images: Walter Bibikow (c). **113** DK Images: Courtesy of the City Museum, Sisak, Croatia (br). **114** Topfoto.co.uk: The British Museum, London / HIP (c). **115** akg-images: Archives CDA / Guillot (t). The Art Archive: Archaeological Museum Naples / Dagli Orti (b). **117** akg-images: Erich Lessing (t). The Art Archive: Musée du Louvre Paris / Dagli Orti (br). **118** www.bridgeman.co.uk: Musee des Pays de L'Ain, Bourg-en-Bresse, France, Lauros / Giraudon (b). **119** The Art Archive: (br); Victoria and Albert Museum London / Eileen Tweedy (tr). **120** DK Images: Courtesy of the Natural History Museum, London (tl), (cl). **121** DK Images: The British Museum, London (bl). Lonely Planet Images: John Elk III (tr). **122** The Art Archive: Museo Prenestino Palestrina / Dagli Orti (cbr). Lonely Planet Images: George Tsafos. **123** Corbis: Archivo Iconografico, S.A. (cb). **124** akg-images: (tl). **124-125** The Art Archive: Museo Prenestino Palestrina / Dagli Orti (b). **125** The Art Archive: Dagli Orti (tr). **126** The Art Archive: Archaeological Museum Naples / Dagli Orti (l). **126-127** Lonely Planet Images: Neil Wilson (b). **127** akg-images: Erich Lessing (r). **128-129** The Art Archive: The British Museum, London / Eileen Tweedy (tl); Museo Capitolino Rome / Dagli Orti. **129** Corbis: Archivo Iconografico, S.A (cr). **130** DK Images: Courtesy of the National Archaeological Museum, Athens (b). **131** Corbis: Richard List (tl). **132-133** DK Images: The British Museum, London. **134** www.bridgeman.co.uk: The British Museum, London, UK, (bl). **135** The Art Archive: Archaeological Museum Paestum / Dagli Orti (tr). © Michael Holford: (bl). University Of Manchester: (cr). **136** Corbis: Roger Wood (bl). DK Images: Glasgow Museum (tr). The Art Archive: Musée du Louvre Paris / Dagli Orti (ca). **137** Corbis: Arte & Immagini srl (cb). The Art Archive: Archaeological Museum Naples / Dagli Orti (tc). Mary Evans Picture Library: (br). **138** Corbis: Roger Wood (bl); Wolfgang Kaehler (tr). **139** The Art Archive: The British Museum, London / Eileen Tweedy (c).

All other images © Dorling Kindersley
For further information see: www.dkimages.com

Dorling Kindersley would also like to thank: Ben Hoare for editorial assistance; and Chris Bernstein for the index.